THE VERY BEST OF

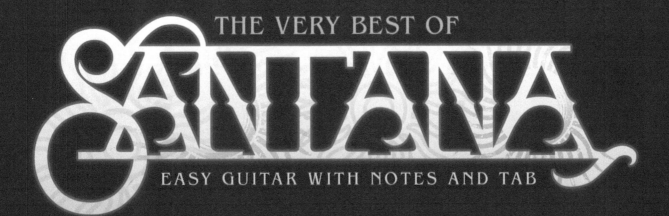

SANTANA

EASY GUITAR WITH NOTES AND TAB

T0065902

Cover photo by Maryanne Bilham

ISBN 978-1-4950-7022-8

7777 W. BLUEMOUND RD. P.O. BOX 13819 MILWAUKEE, WI 53213

Visit Hal Leonard Online at
www.halleonard.com

STRUM AND PICK PATTERNS

This chart contains the suggested strum and pick patterns that are referred to by number at the beginning of each song in this book. The symbols ⊓ and ∨ in the strum patterns refer to down and up strokes, respectively. The letters in the pick patterns indicate which right-hand fingers play which strings.

p = thumb
i = index finger
m = middle finger
a = ring finger

For example; Pick Pattern 2
is played: thumb - index - middle - ring

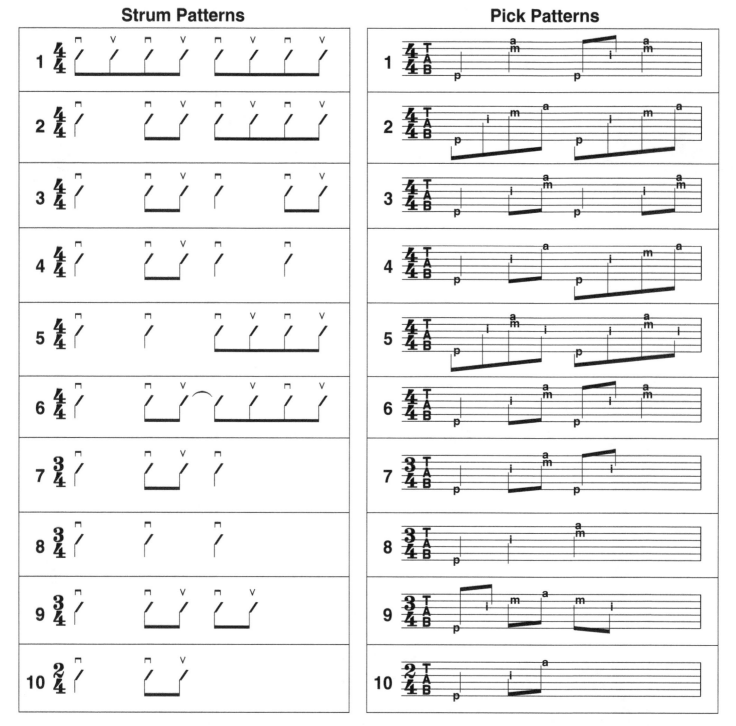

You can use the 3/4 Strum and Pick Patterns in songs written in compound meter (6/8, 9/8, 12/8, etc.).
For example, you can accompany a song in 6/8 by playing the 3/4 pattern twice in each measure.
The 4/4 Strum and Pick Patterns can be used for songs written in cut time (¢) by doubling the note time values in the patterns. Each pattern would therefore last two measures in cut time.

CONTENTS

Black Magic Woman

Words and Music by Peter Green

Dm   Am   Gm   A7

Strum Pattern: 3
Pick Pattern: 3

Verse

Moderately

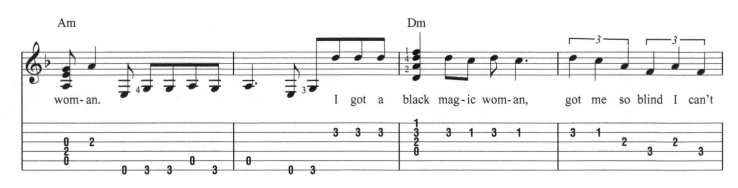

1. Got a black mag-ic wom-an, got a black mag-ic

2., 3. *See additional lyrics*

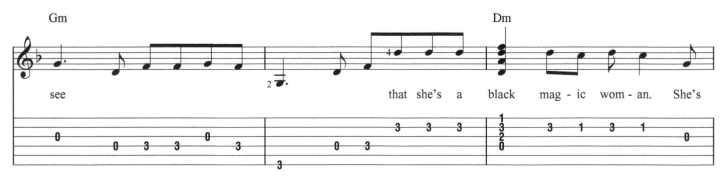

wom-an. I got a black mag-ic wom-an, got me so blind I can't

see that she's a black mag-ic wom-an. She's

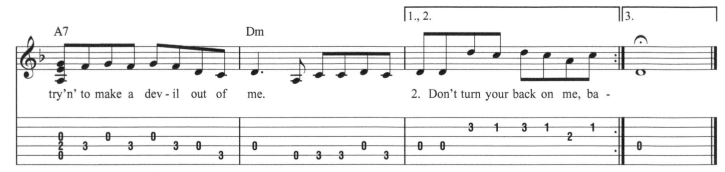

try'n' to make a dev-il out of me.

1., 2. 2. Don't turn your back on me, ba-

3.

Additional Lyrics

2. Don't turn your back on me, baby,
Don't turn your back on me, baby.
Yes, don't turn your back on me, baby,
Stop messin' 'round with your tricks.
Don't turn your back on me, baby,
You just might pick up my magic sticks.

3. You got your spell on me, baby,
You got your spell on me, baby.
Yes, you got your spell on me, baby,
Turnin' my heart into stone.
I need you so bad,
Magic woman, I can't leave you alone.

Europa

Words and Music by Carlos Santana and Tom Coster

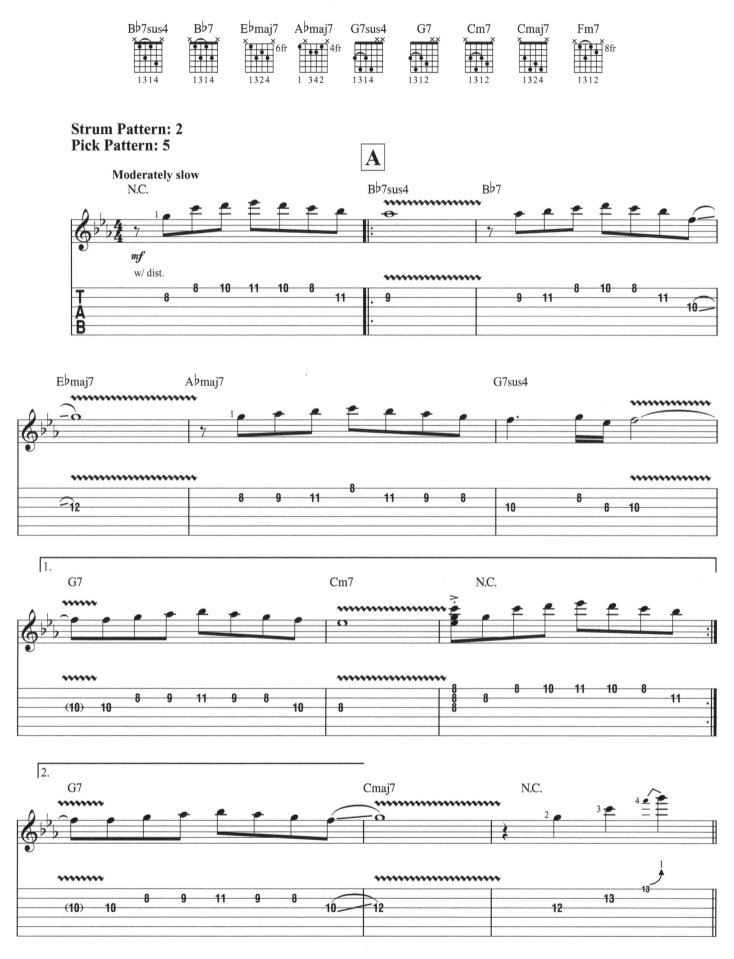

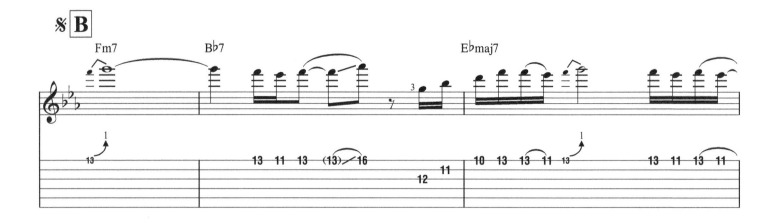

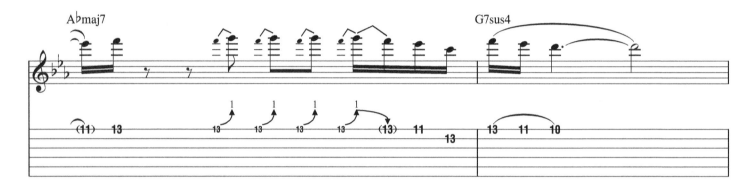

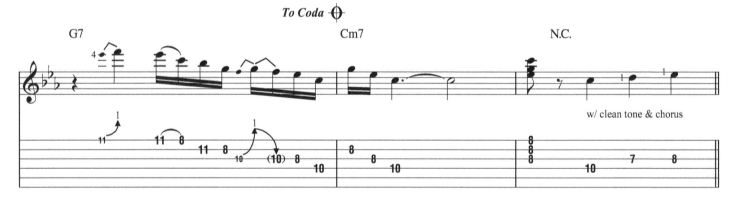

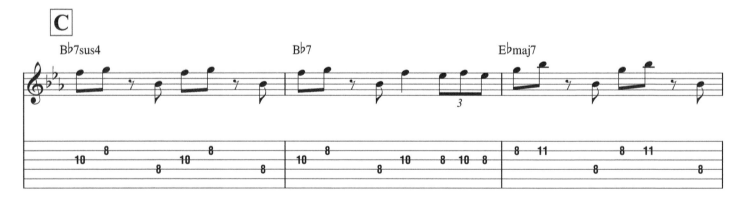

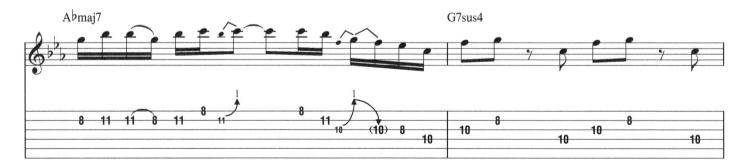

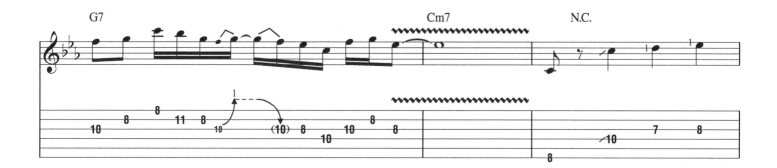

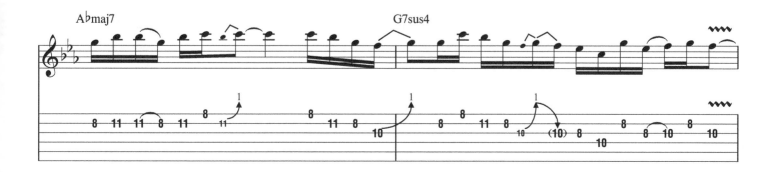

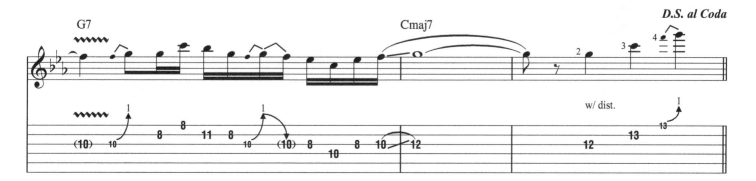

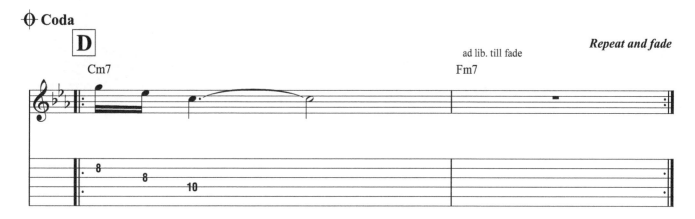

Corazon Espinado

Words and Music by Fher Sierra

*Capo II

Strum Pattern: 3
Pick Pattern: 3

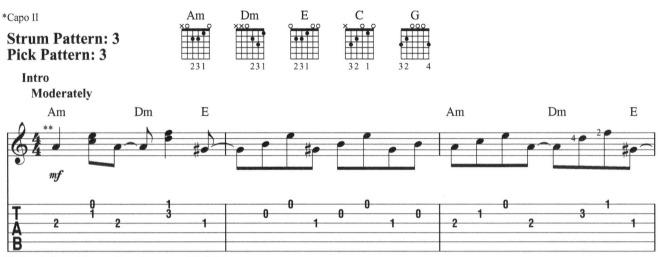

Intro
Moderately

*Optional: To match recording, place capo at 2nd fret.
**Piano arr. for gtr., next 4 meas.

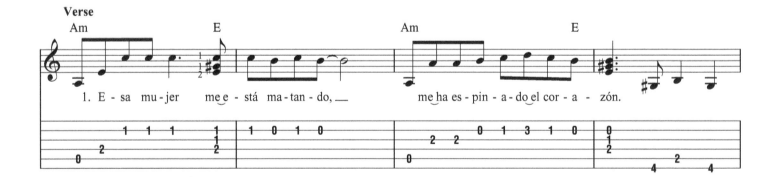

Play 4 times

Verse

1. E - sa mu - jer me e - stá ma - tan - do, __ me ha es - pin - a - do el cor - a - zón.

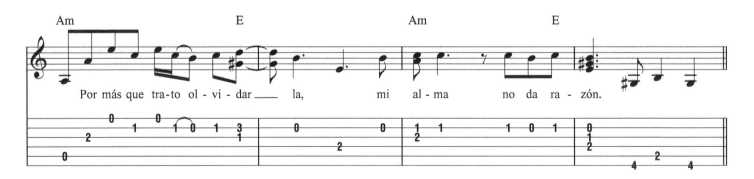

Por más que tra - to ol - vi - dar __ la, mi al - ma no da ra - zón.

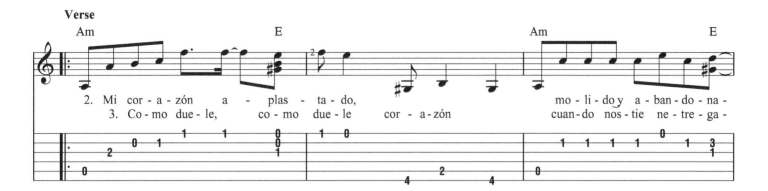

Verse

2. Mi cor - a - zón a - plas - ta - do, mo - li - do y a - ban - do - na -
3. Co - mo due - le, co - mo due - le cor - a - zón cuan - do nos tie - ne - tre - ga -

- do. A ver, a ver, tu sa - bes, di - me mi a - mor, __ por fa -
- dos. Pe - ro no ol - vi - des, mu - jer, que al - gún dí - a di - rás, __ "Ay, ay,

Chorus

vor. He que do - lor nos que - dó. __ Ah, ah, ay, __
ay! Co - mo me due - le el a - mor." __

__ cor - a - zón es - pi - na - do. Co - mo due - le, me due - le, ma - má. __ Ah, ah, ay, _

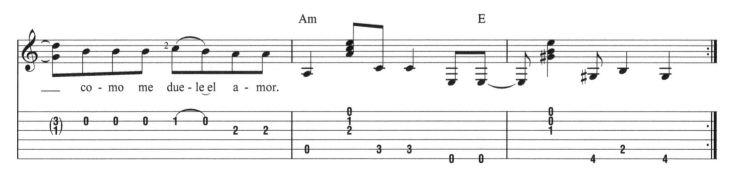

__ co - mo me due - le el a - mor.

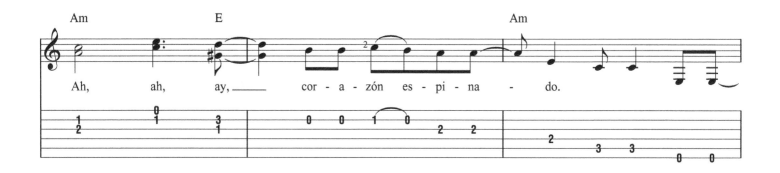

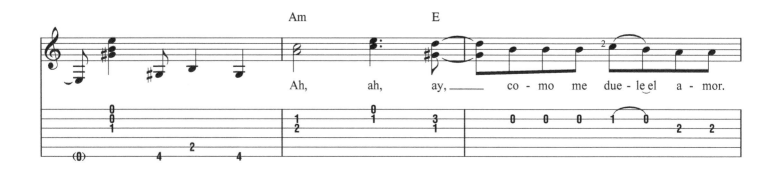

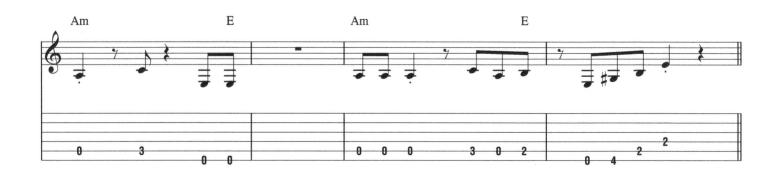

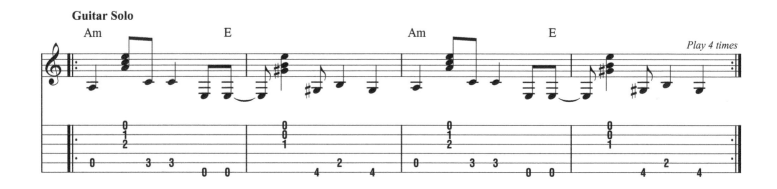

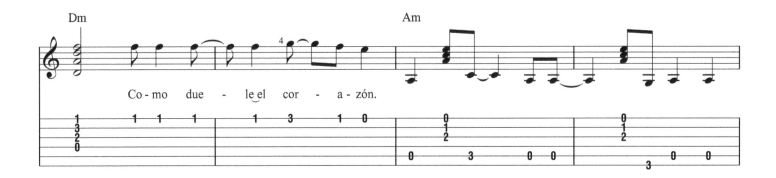

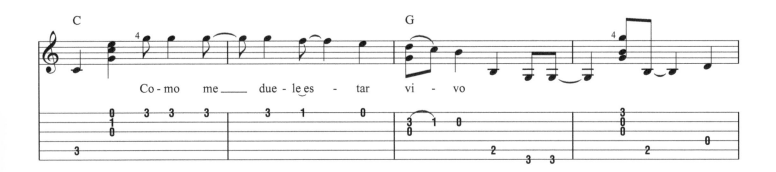

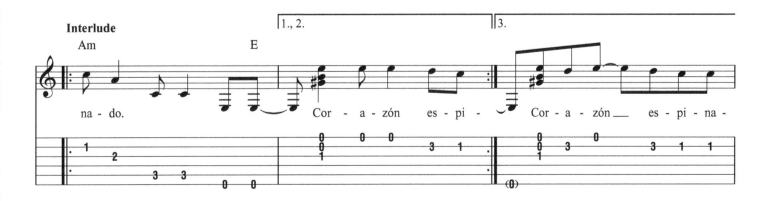

Outro-Guitar Solo

Repeat and fade

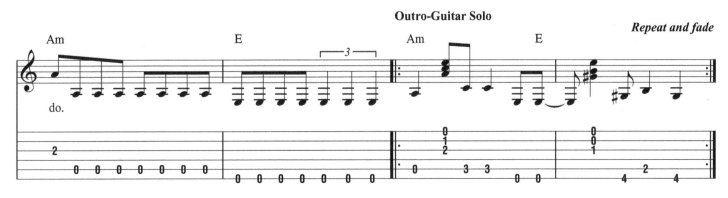

Everybody's Everything

Words by Carlos Santana
Music by Tyrone Moss and Milton Brown

*Optional: To match recording, place capo at 1st fret.

Sing - in' round, sing - in' round, for ev - 'ry - one. ___
Sing it loud, time for you to all get down. ___

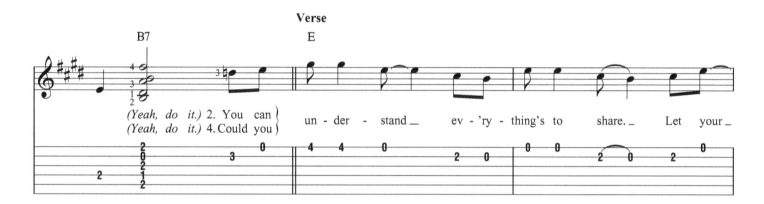

Verse

(Yeah, do it.) 2. You can
(Yeah, do it.) 4. Could you
un - der - stand ___ ev - 'ry - thing's to share. ___ Let your ___

___ spir - it dance, ___ broth - ers, ev - 'ry - where. ___ Let your ___ head be free, ___ turn the

wis - dom key. ___ Find it ___ nat - 'ral - ly, ___ see you're luck - y to be. ___

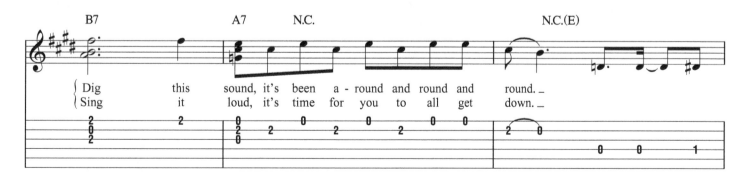

Dig this sound, it's been a - round and round and round. ___
Sing it loud, it's time for you to all get down. ___

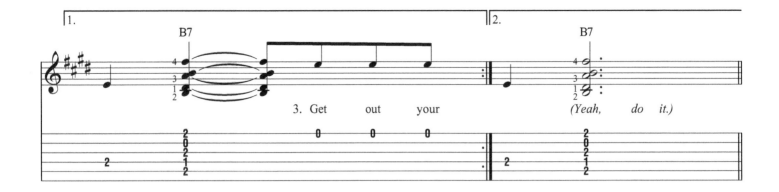

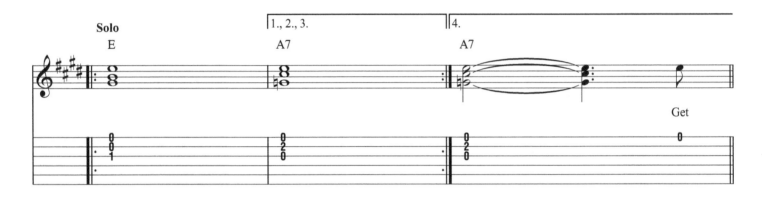

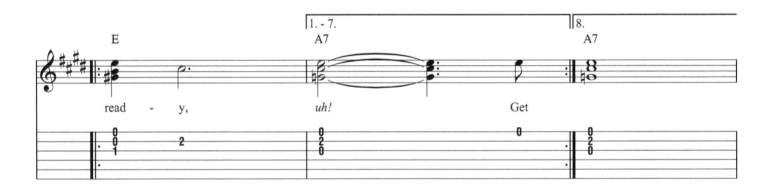

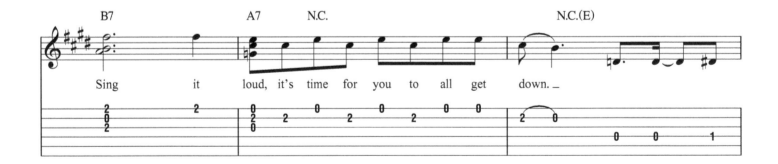

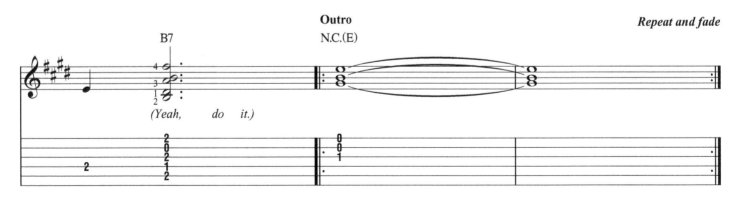

Oye Como Va

Words and Music by Tito Puente

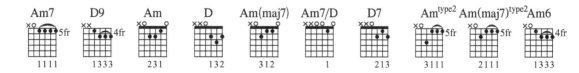

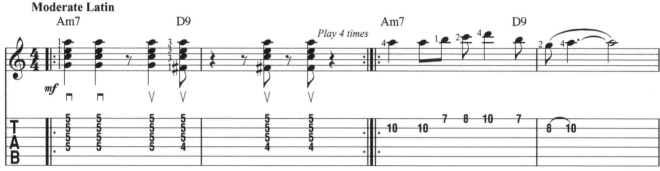

Strum Pattern: 2
Pick Pattern: 2

Intro
Moderate Latin

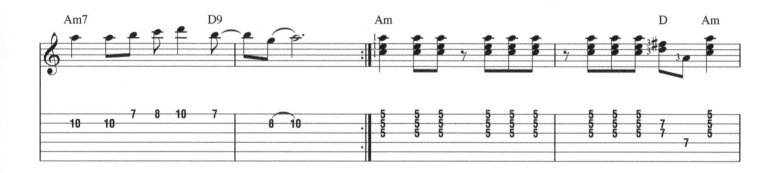

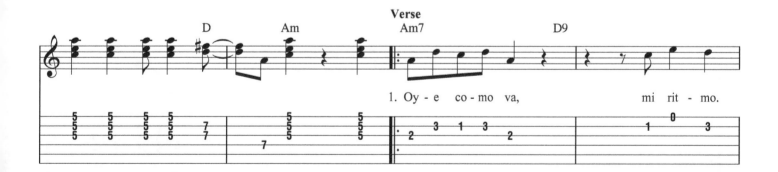

1. Oy - e co - mo va,   mi rit - mo.

Bue - no pa go - zar,   mu - la - ta.

Guitar Solo

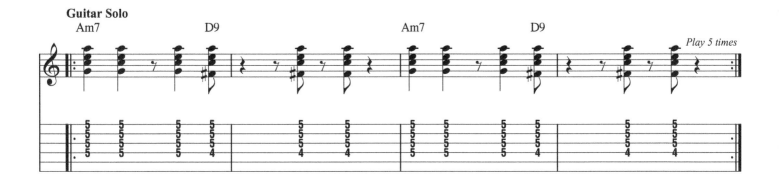

Interlude

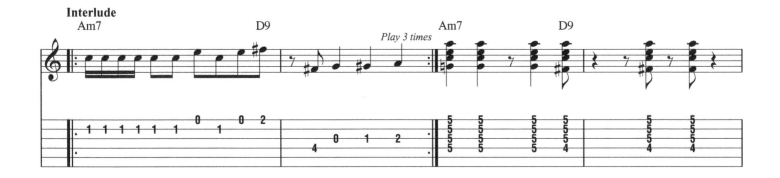

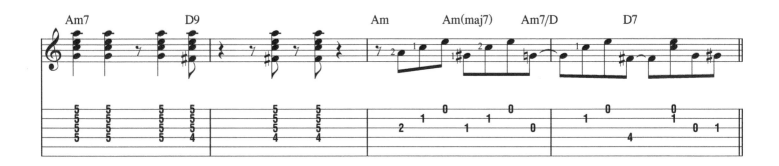

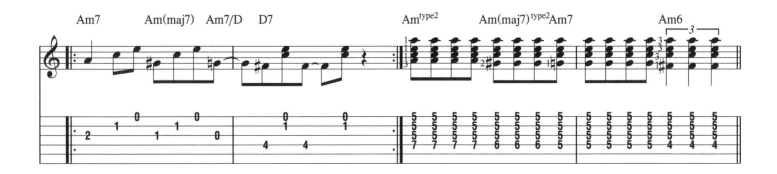

Organ Solo　　　　　　　　　　　　　　　　**Bridge**

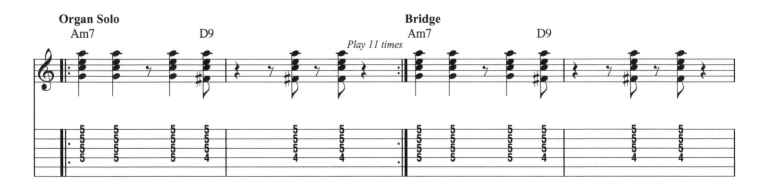

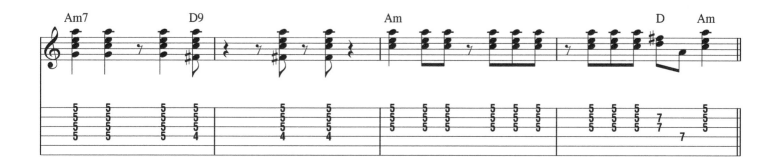

Verse

2. Oy - e co - mo va,   mi rit - mo. Bue - no pa go - zar,   mu - la - ta.

Breakdown

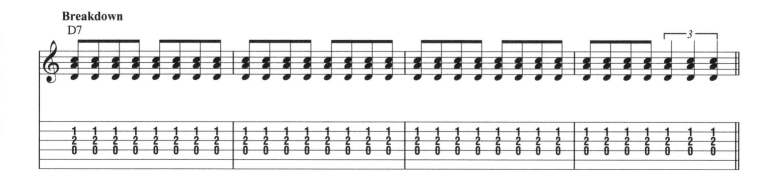

Guitar Solo

Play 6 times

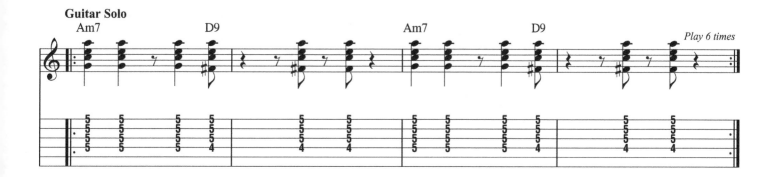

Outro

Uhh!

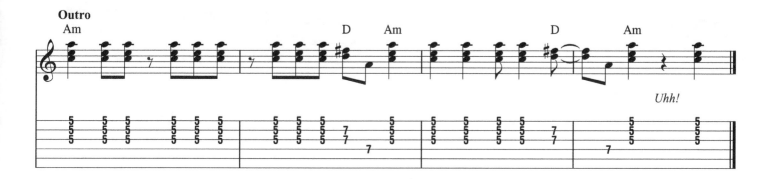

Evil Ways

Words and Music by Sonny Henry

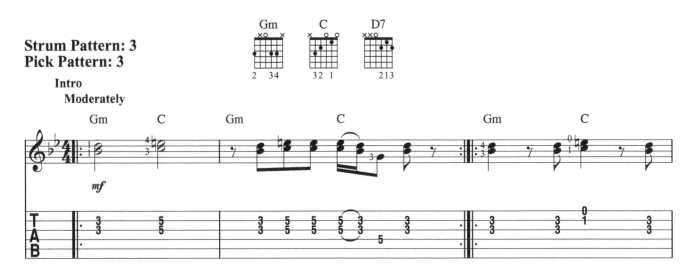

Strum Pattern: 3
Pick Pattern: 3

Intro
Moderately

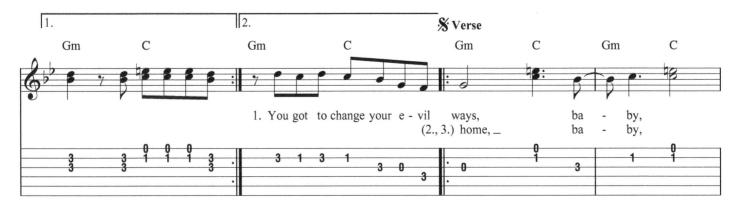

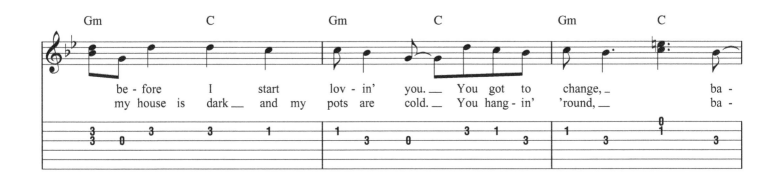

1. You got to change your e-vil ways, ba-by,
(2., 3.) home,__ ba-by,

be-fore I start lov-in' you.__ You got to change,__ ba-by,
my house is dark__ and my pots are cold. You hang-in' 'round,__ ba-

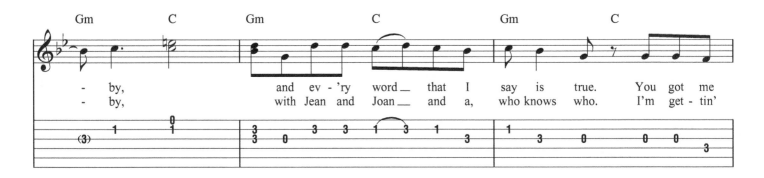

- by, and ev-'ry word__ that I say is true. You got me
- by, with Jean and Joan__ and a, who knows who. I'm get-tin'

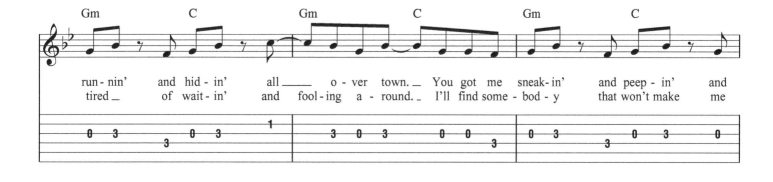

run - nin' and hid - in' all ___ o - ver town. ___ You got me sneak - in' and peep - in' and
tired ___ of wait - in' and fool - ing a - round. ___ I'll find some - bod - y that won't make me

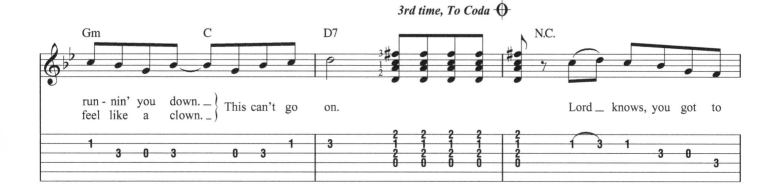

3rd time, To Coda

run - nin' you down. ___ } This can't go on. Lord ___ knows, you got to
feel like a clown. ___ }

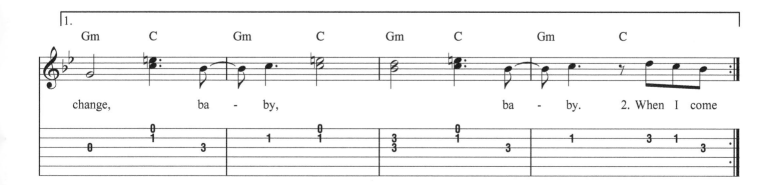

1.

change, ba - by, ba - by. 2. When I come

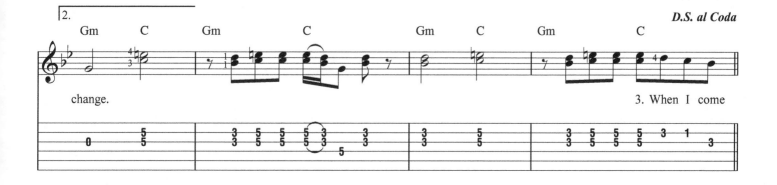

2.

D.S. al Coda

change. 3. When I come

Coda   **Outro-Guitar Solo**   *Repeat and fade*

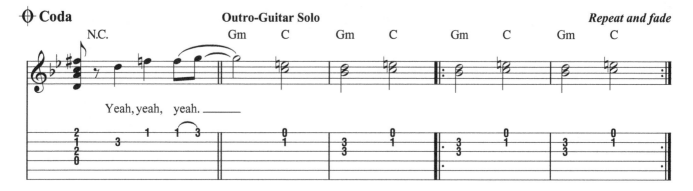

Yeah, yeah, yeah. _____

The Game of Love

Words and Music by Rick Nowels and Gregg Alexander

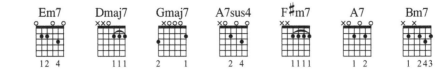

Strum Pattern: 3, 6
Pick Pattern: 4, 5

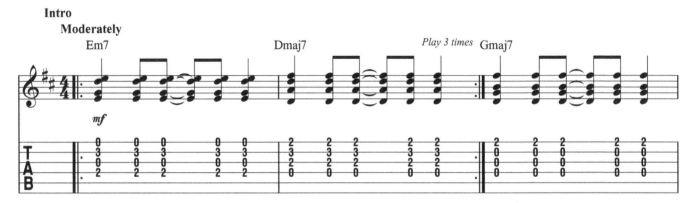

*Female vocal sung one octave higher than written.

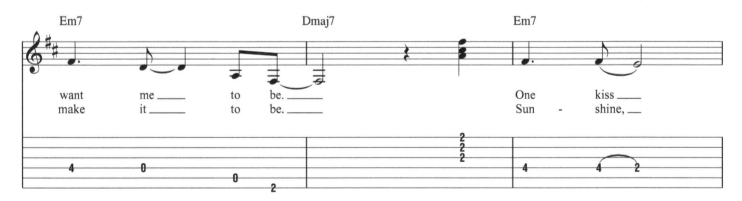

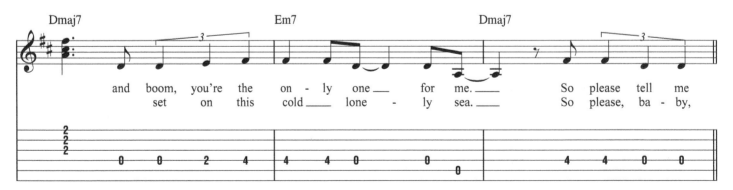

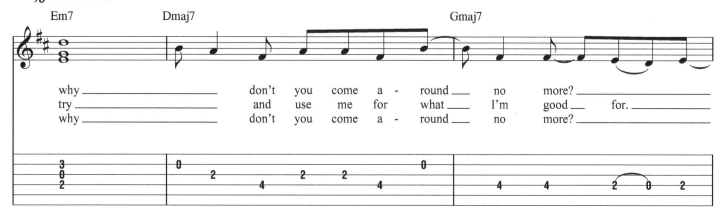

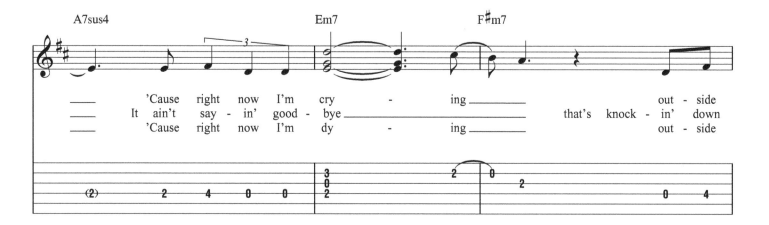

Chorus

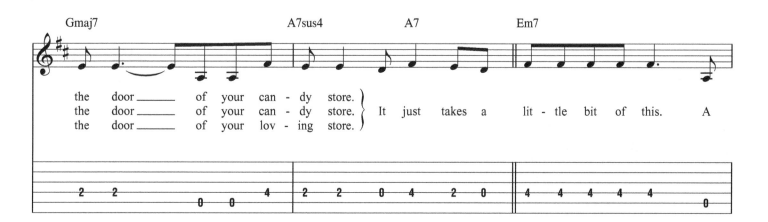

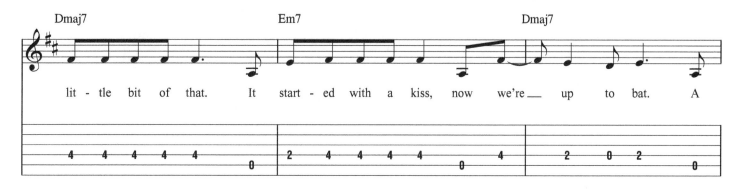

lit - tle bit of laughs. A lit - tle bit of pain. I'm tell - ing you my babe, it's all __

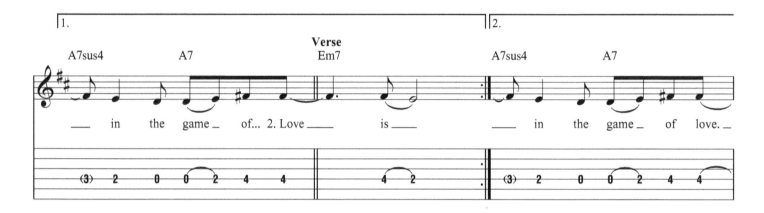

__ in the game __ of... 2. Love __ is __ __ in the game __ of love. __

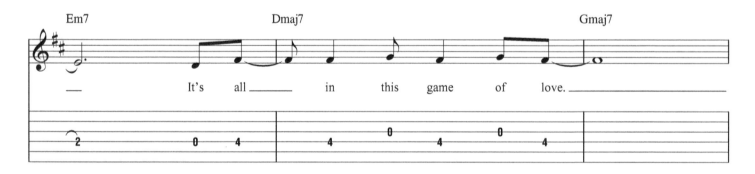

__ It's all __ in this game of love. __

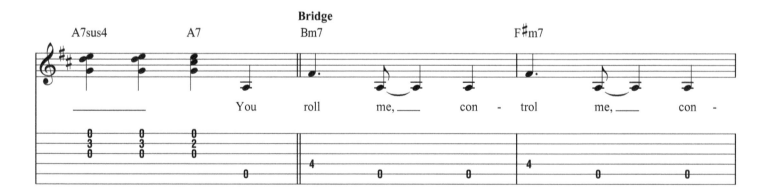

__ You roll me, __ con - trol me, __ con -

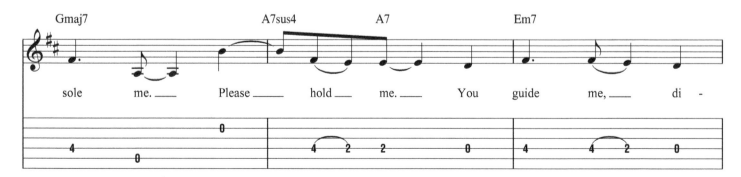

sole me. __ Please __ hold __ me. __ You guide me, __ di -

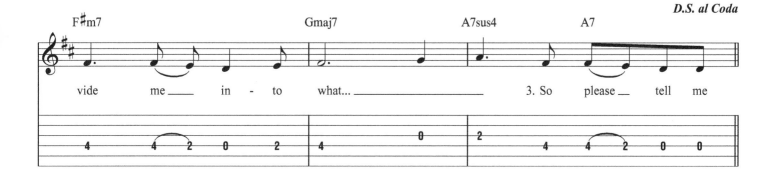

vide me ___ in - to what... ___ 3. So please ___ tell me

Coda

Outro

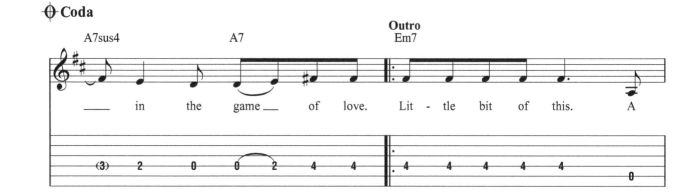

___ in the game ___ of love. Lit - tle bit of this. A

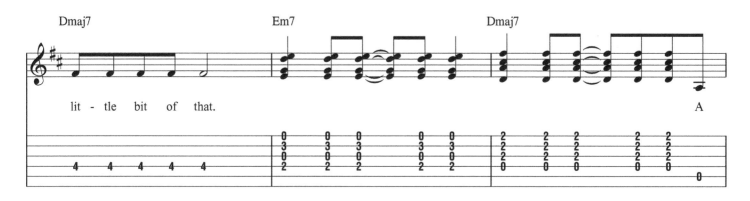

lit - tle bit of that. A

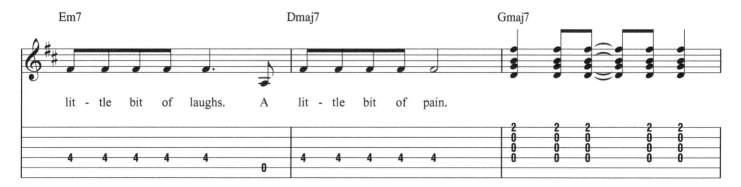

lit - tle bit of laughs. A lit - tle bit of pain.

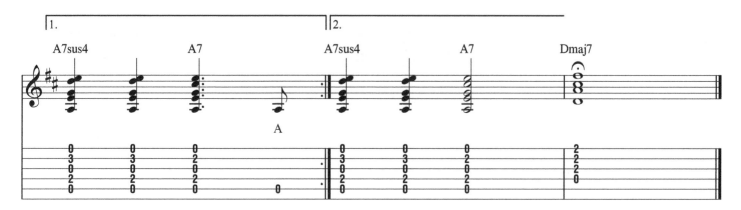

A

Into the Night

Words and Music by Chad Kroeger

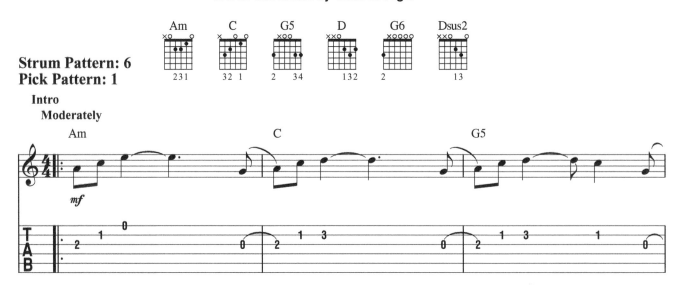

Strum Pattern: 6
Pick Pattern: 1

Intro
Moderately

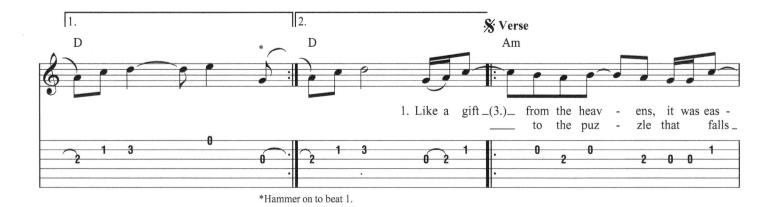

*Hammer on to beat 1.

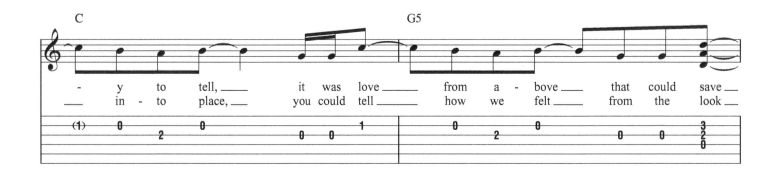

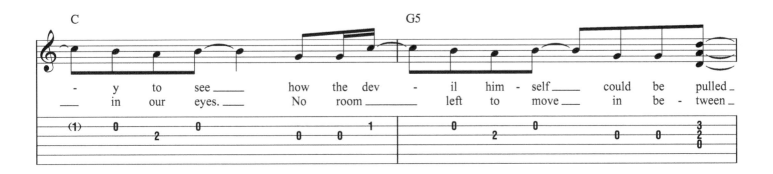

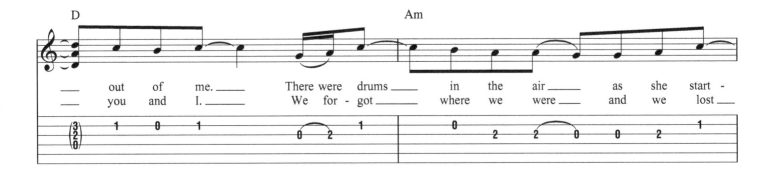

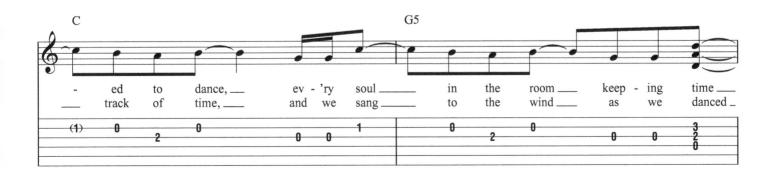

Chorus

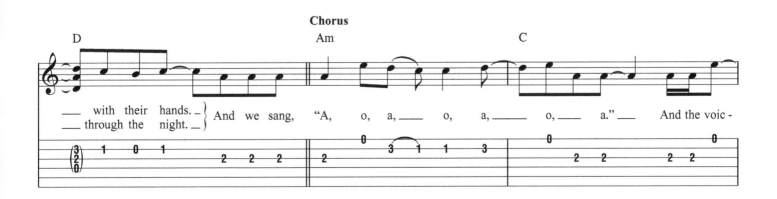

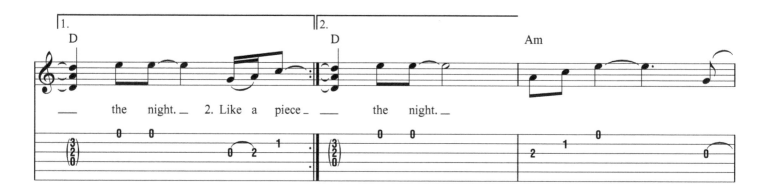

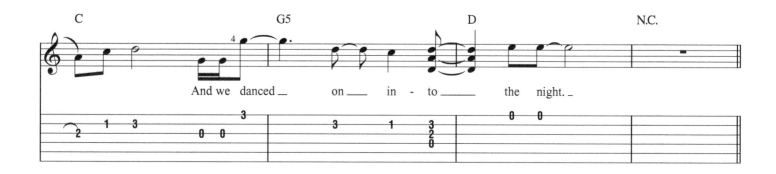

Guitar Solo

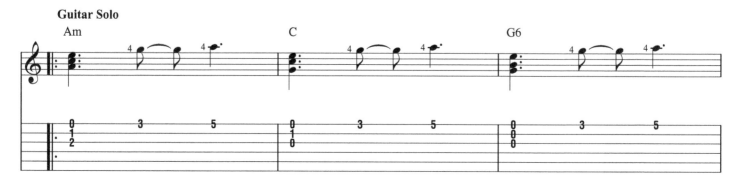

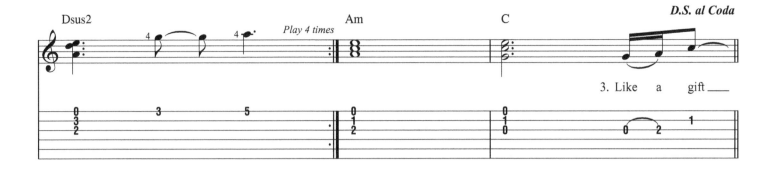

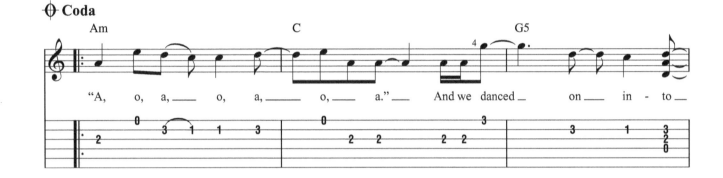

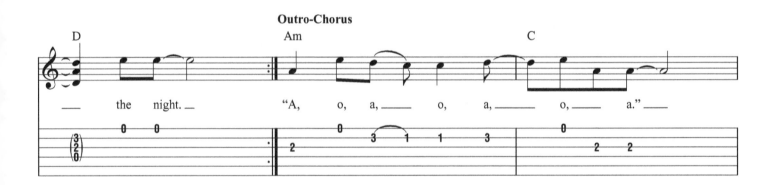

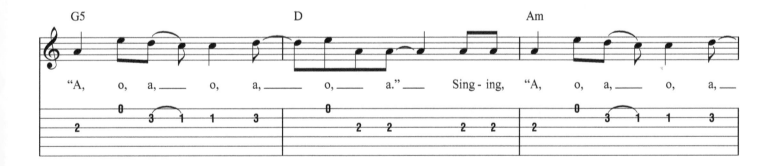

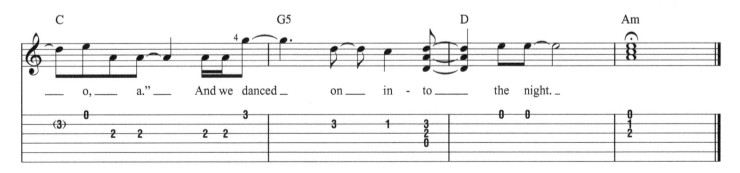

Love of My Life

Words and Music by Carlos Santana and Dave Matthews

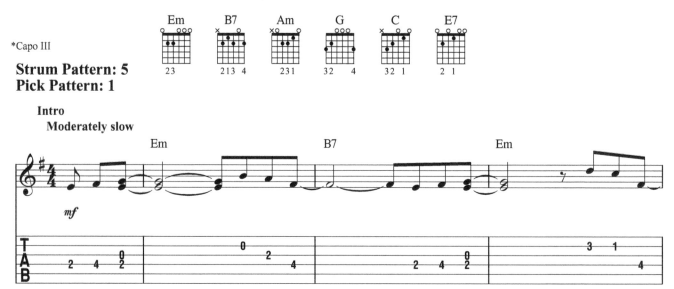

*Capo III

Strum Pattern: 5
Pick Pattern: 1

Intro
Moderately slow

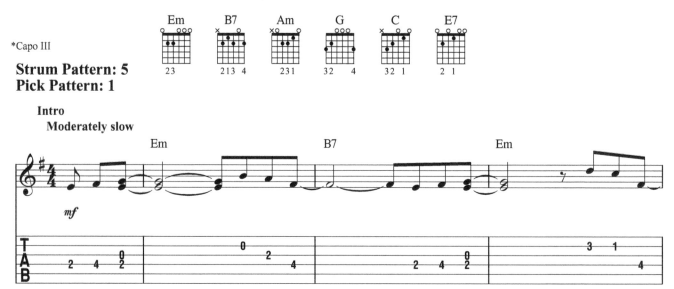

*Optional: To match recording, place capo at 3rd fret.

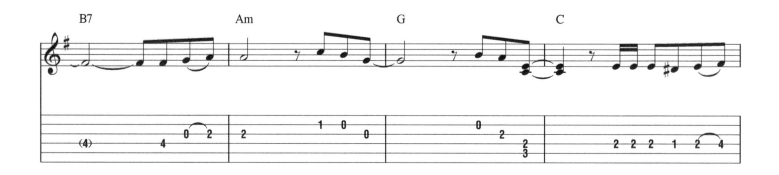

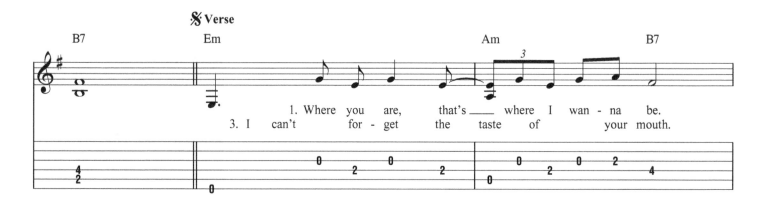

1. Where you are, that's ___ where I wan - na be.
3. I can't for - get the taste of your mouth.

And through your eyes all ___ the things I wan - na see.
From your lips all the heav - ens pour out. ___

And in the night ___
I can't for - get when, ah,

you are my dream. You're ev - 'ry - thing to me. ____
we are one. You a - lone ____ I am free. ____

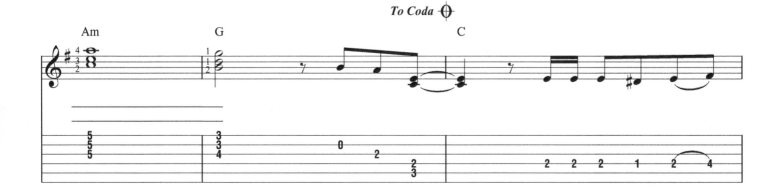

To Coda ⊕

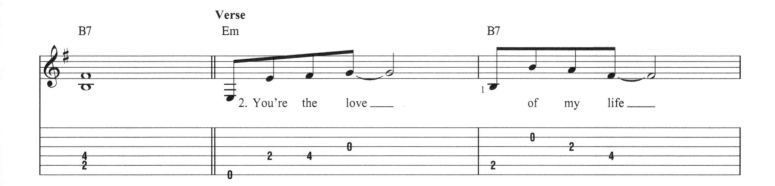

Verse

2. You're the love ____ of my life ____

and the breath ____ in my prayers. ____ Take my hand ____

D.S. al Coda

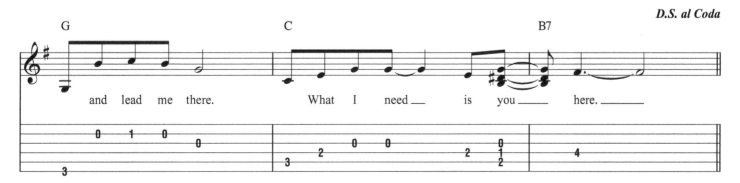

and lead me there. What I need ____ is you ____ here. ____

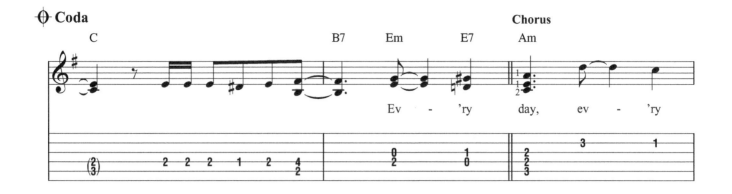

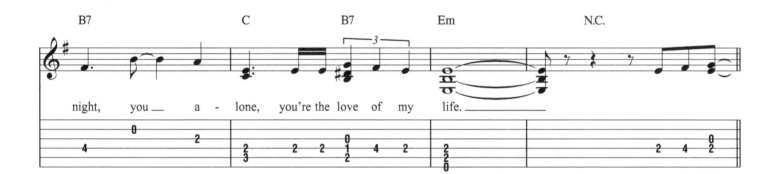

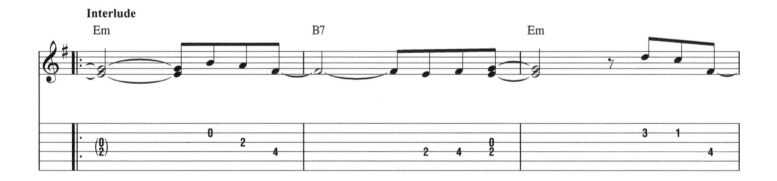

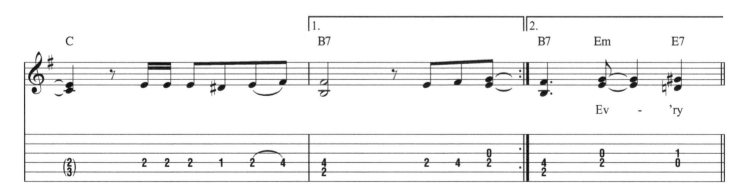

Chorus

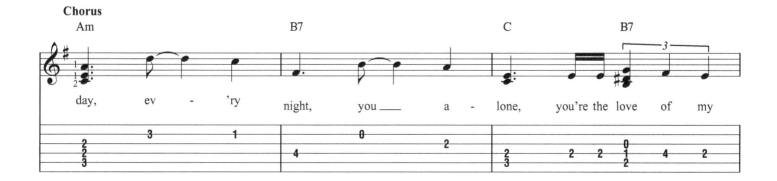

day, ev - 'ry night, you ___ a - lone, you're the love of my

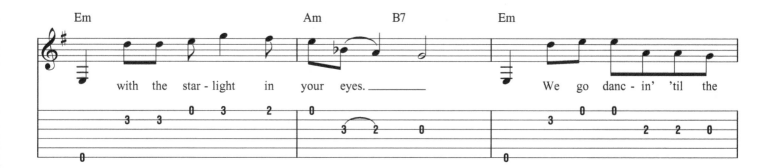

life. ___ We go danc - in' in the moon - light, ___

Bridge

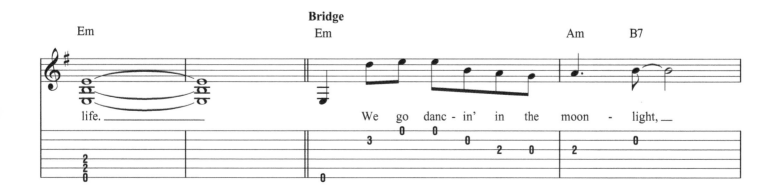

with the star - light in your eyes. ___ We go danc - in' 'til the

sun - rise. ___ You and me, we're gon - na dance, dance, ___ dance. ___

Outro-Guitar Solo

Repeat and fade

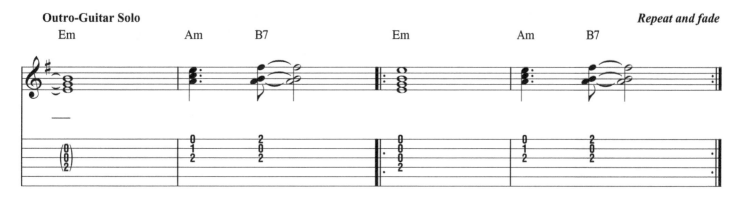

Maria Maria

Words and Music by Wyclef Jean, Jerry Duplessis, Carlos Santana, Karl Perazzo, Paul Rekow, Marvin Hough and David McRae

Strum Pattern: 5
Pick Pattern: 5

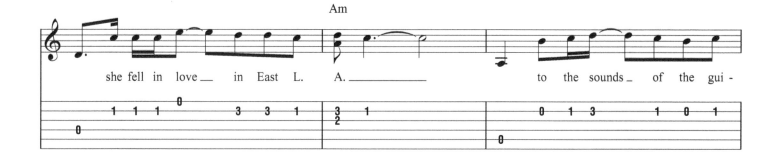

she fell in love ___ in East L. A. _____

to the sounds ___ of the gui-

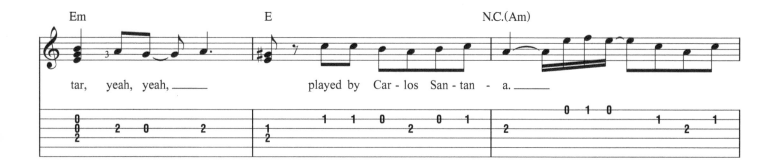

tar,   yeah, yeah, _____

played by Car - los San - tan - a. _____

3rd time, To Coda

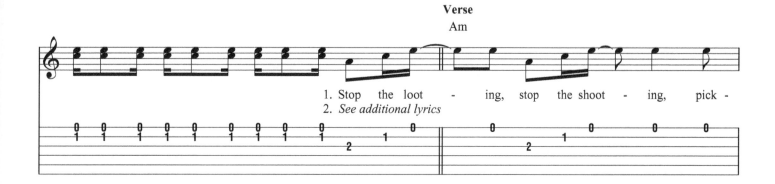

Verse

1. Stop   the   loot   -   ing,   stop   the   shoot   -   ing,   pick -
2. *See additional lyrics*

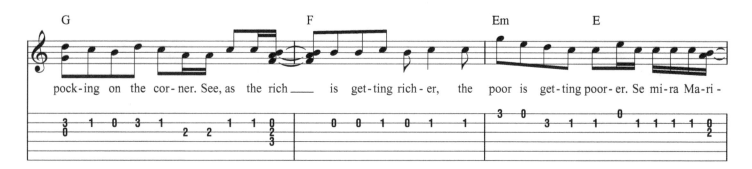

pock-ing on the cor-ner. See, as the rich ___ is get-ting rich-er,   the   poor is get-ting poor-er. Se mi-ra Ma-ri-

- a on the cor-ner, think-ing of ways _ to make it bet-ter. In my mail - box there's an e-vic - tion let-ter.

Interlude

Some-bod-y just _ said see you lat-er. *(Ahora vengo mama chola mama chola. Ahora vengo mama chola. A-*

hora vengo mama chola mama chola. A-hora vengo...) Ma-ri - a, Ma-ri - *hora vengo mama chola. A-*

hora vengo mama chola mama chola. Ahora vengo mama chola. Ahora vengo mama chola mama chola. A-

Bridge

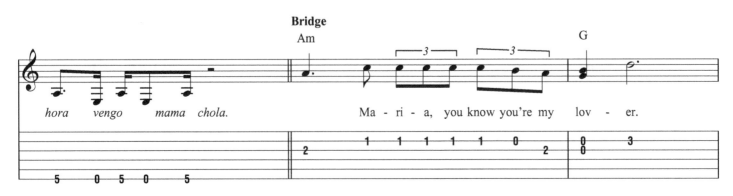

hora vengo mama chola. Ma-ri - a, you know you're my lov - er.

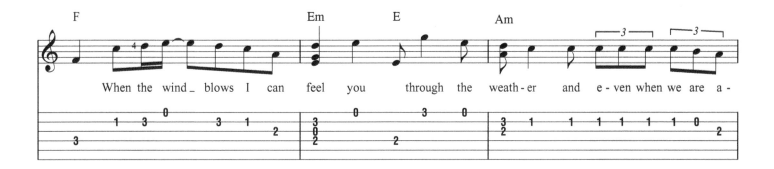

When the wind _ blows I can feel you through the weath-er and e-ven when we are a-

part, _____ still feels like we're to-geth - er. Ma - ri -

Coda

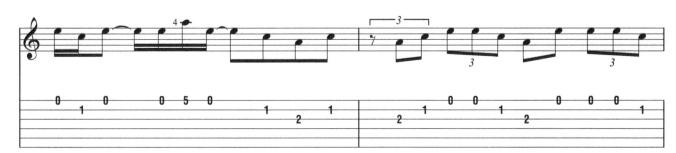

Outro

N.C.(Am)

Repeat and fade

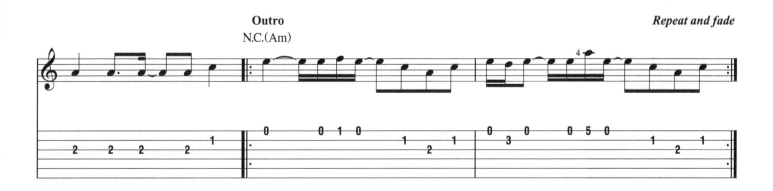

Additional Lyrics

2. I said a la favella los colores.
   The streets are getting hotter.
   There is no water to put out the fire.
   Mi canto la esperanza.
   Se mira Maria on the corner,
   Thinking of ways to make it better.
   Then I looked up in the sky
   Hoping of days of paradise.

No One to Depend On

Words and Music by Gregg Rolie, Michael Carabello and Thomas Escovedo

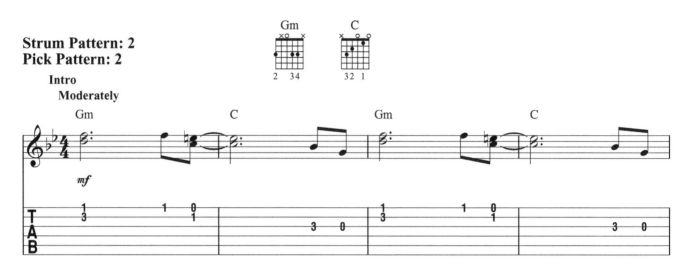

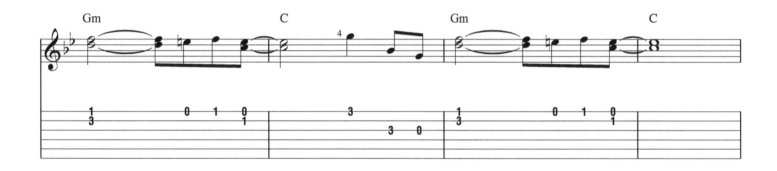

got no-bod-y that I can de-pend on.

Interlude

Verse

2. Ain't got no-bod-y that I can de-

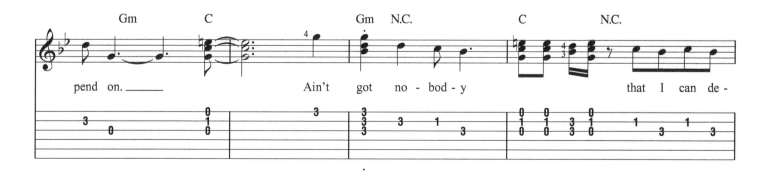

pend on. _____ Ain't got no-bod-y that I can de-

Interlude

w/ Verse 1 pattern

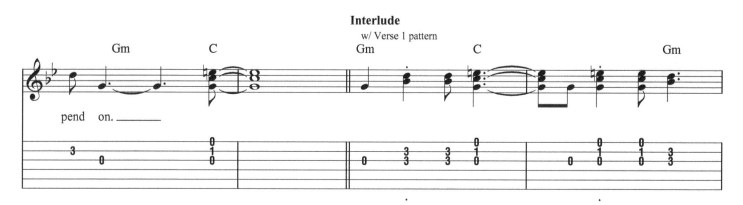

pend on. _____

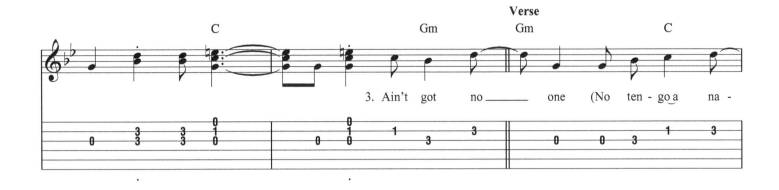

Verse

3. Ain't got no _____ one (No ten-go a na-

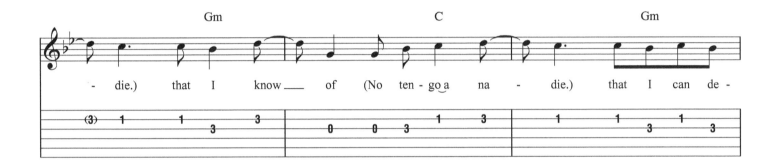

-die.) that I know _____ of (No ten-go a na - die.) that I can de-

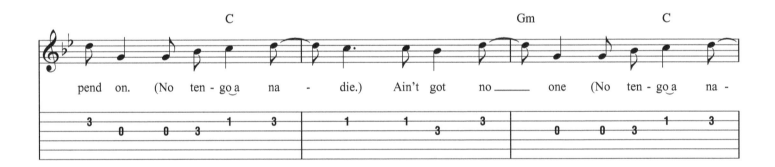

pend on. (No ten-go a na - die.) Ain't got no _____ one (No ten-go a na-

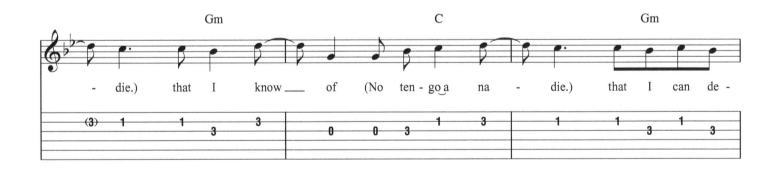

-die.) that I know _____ of (No ten-go a na - die.) that I can de-

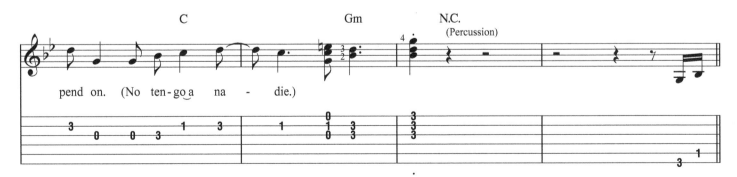

pend on. (No ten-go a na - die.)

38

Bridge

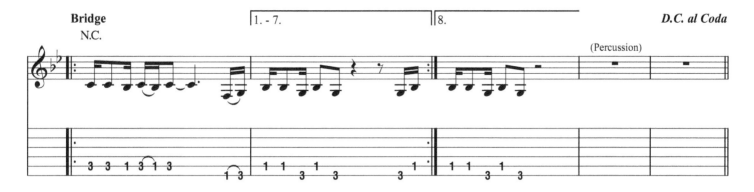

Coda

Verse

w/ Verse 1 pattern

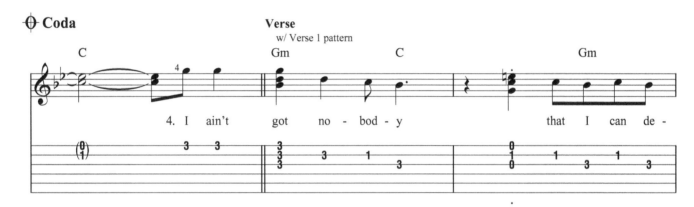

4. I ain't got no - bod - y that I can de -

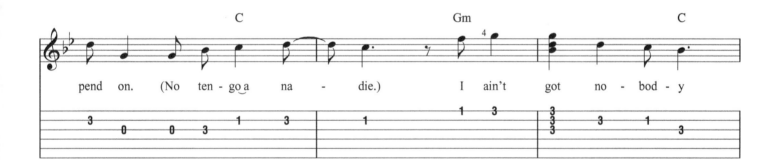

pend on. (No ten - go a na - die.) I ain't got no - bod - y

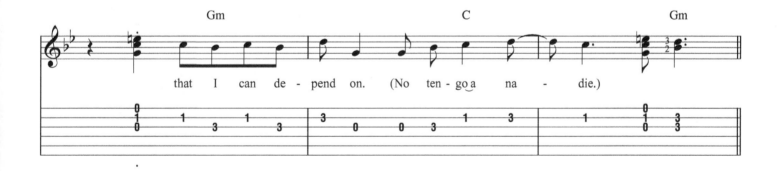

that I can de - pend on. (No ten - go a na - die.)

Outro

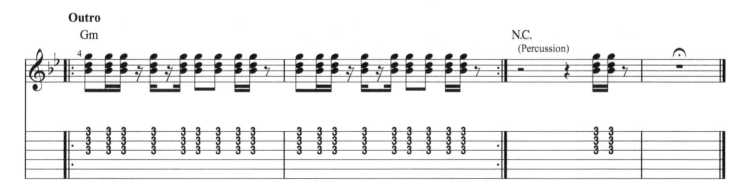

Samba Pa Ti

Words and Music by Carlos Santana

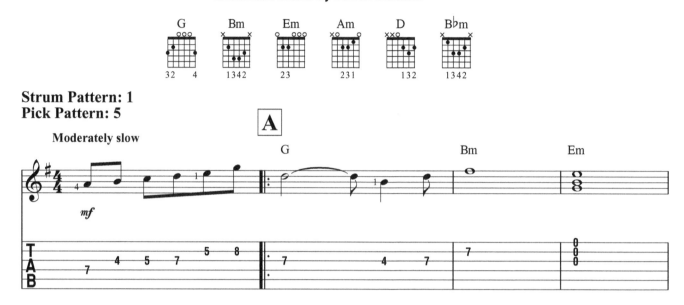

Strum Pattern: 1
Pick Pattern: 5

Moderately slow

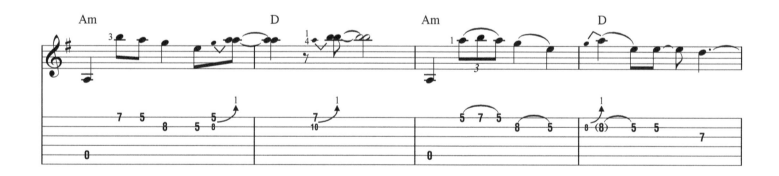

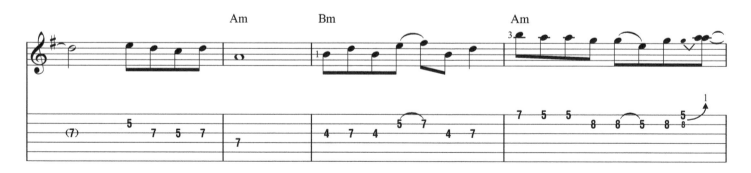

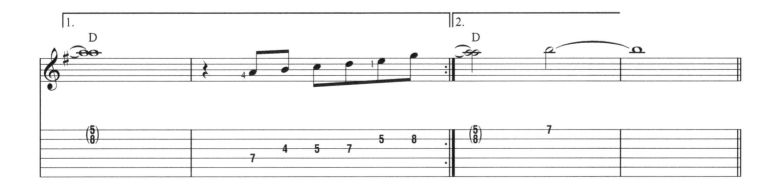

B

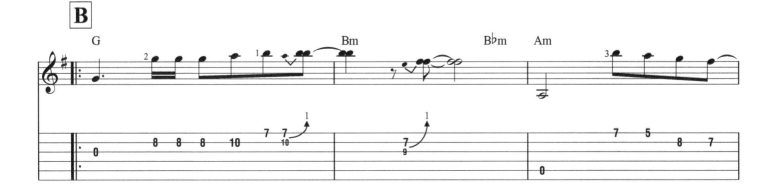

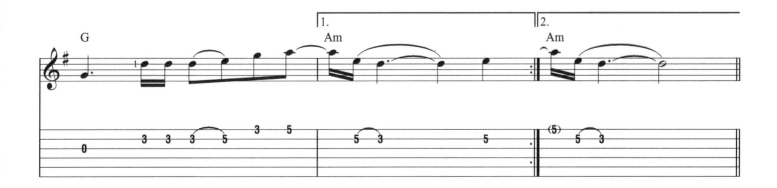

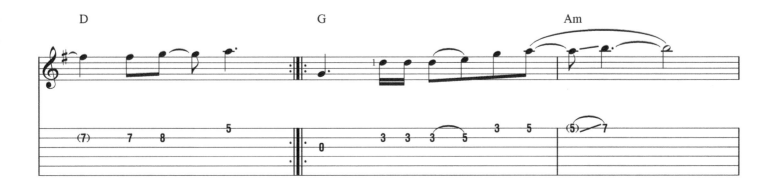

Outro-Guitar Solo

Repeat and fade

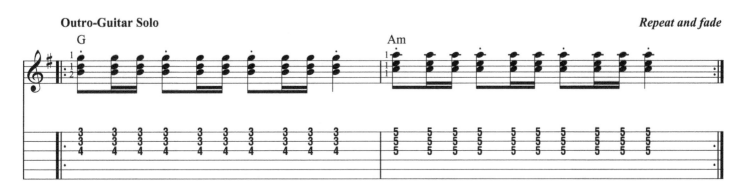

Smooth

Words by Rob Thomas
Music by Rob Thomas and Itaal Shur

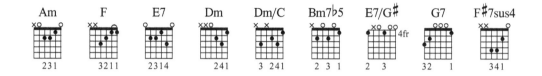

Strum Pattern: 2, 3
Pick Pattern: 3, 4

Intro
Moderately

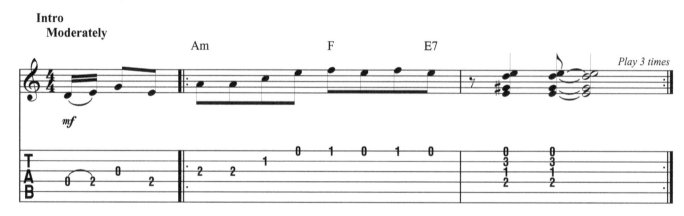

Play 3 times

Verse

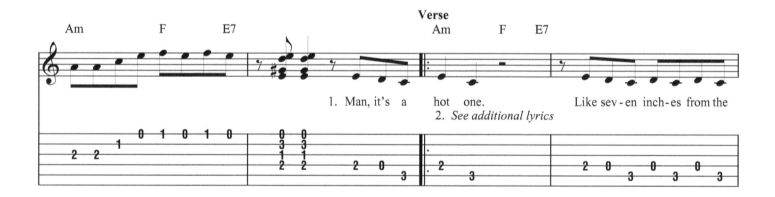

1. Man, it's a   hot one.   Like sev-en inch-es from the
2. *See additional lyrics*

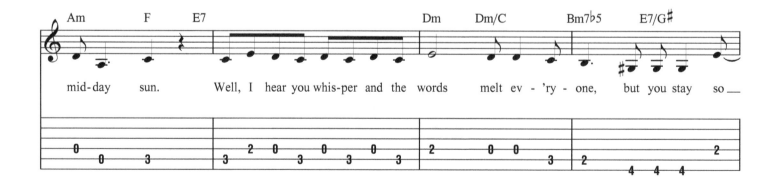

mid-day   sun.   Well, I hear you whis-per and the words   melt ev-'ry-one,   but you stay so ___

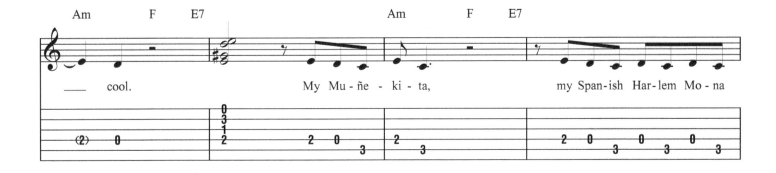

cool. My Mu-ñe-ki-ta, my Span-ish Har-lem Mo-na

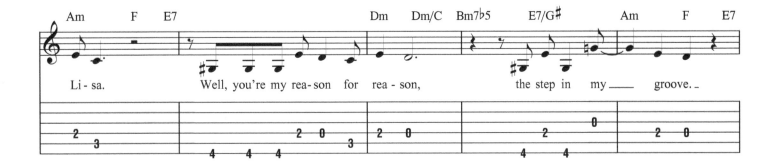

Li-sa. Well, you're my rea-son for rea-son, the step in my ___ groove. ___

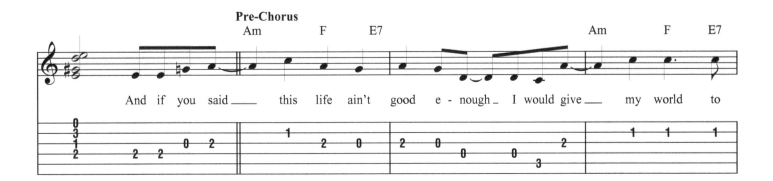

Pre-Chorus

And if you said ___ this life ain't good e-nough ___ I would give ___ my world to

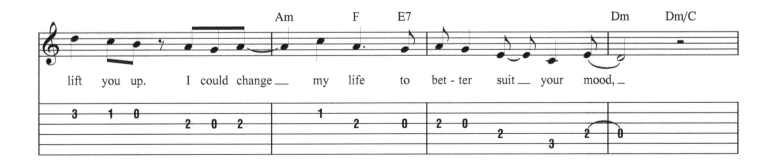

lift you up. I could change ___ my life to bet-ter suit ___ your mood, ___

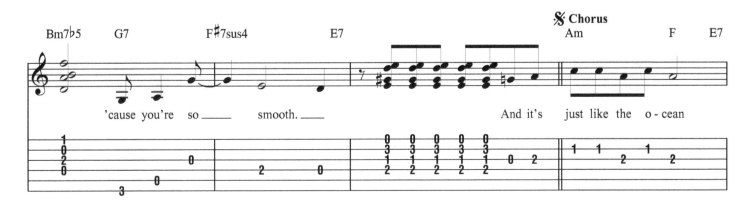

Chorus

'cause you're so ___ smooth. ___ And it's just like the o-cean

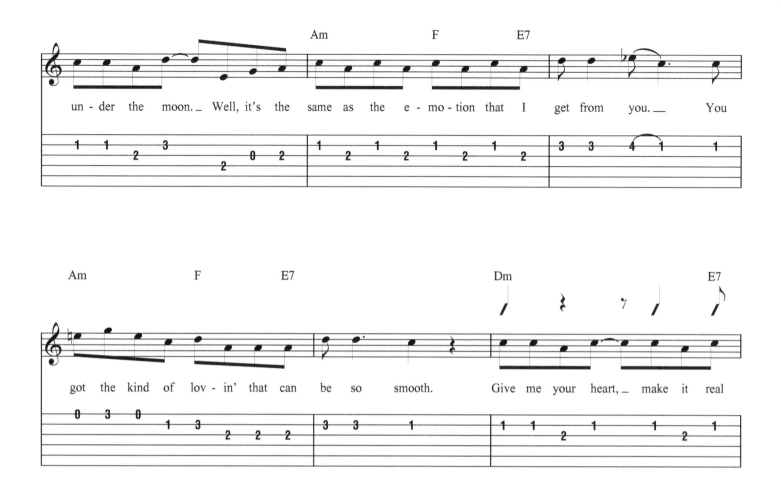

Guitar Solo

D.S. al Coda

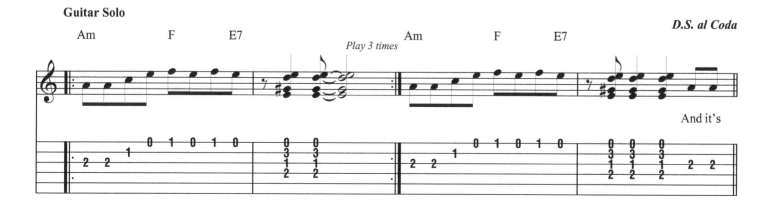

Play 3 times

And it's

Coda
Outro

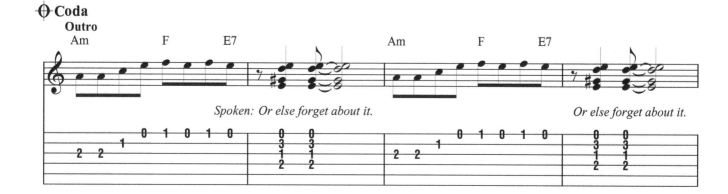

Spoken: Or else forget about it.

Or else forget about it.

Let's don't forget about it. Give me your heart, _ make it real. _

Repeat and fade

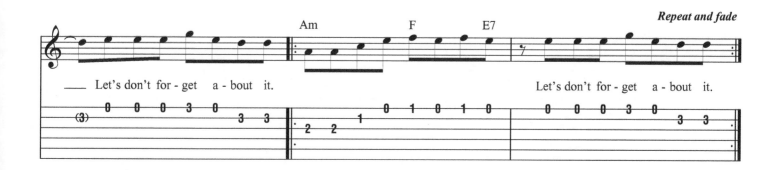

_ Let's don't for - get a - bout it. Let's don't for - get a - bout it.

Additional Lyrics

2. Well, I'll tell you one thing,
If you would leave it'd be a crying shame.
In ev'ry breath and ev'ry word,
I hear your name calling me out.
Out from the barrio,
You hear my rhythm on your radio.
You feel the turning of the world so soft and slow,
Turning me 'round and 'round.

Why Don't You & I

Words and Music by Chad Kroeger

*Capo III

Strum Pattern: 1
Pick Pattern: 5

Intro
Moderately slow

*Optional: To match recording, place capo at 3rd fret.

Verse

1. Since the mo-ment I spot - ted you, like walk - in' 'round with lit - tle wings on my shoes,
2. *See additional lyrics*

my stom - ach's filled with the but - ter - flies, ____ oo, and it's al - right.

Bounc - in' 'round from cloud _ to cloud, I got the feel- in' like I'm nev - er gon- na come down.

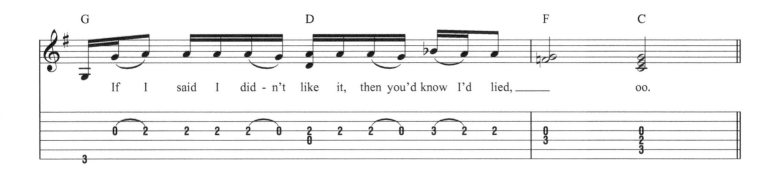

If I said I did - n't like it, then you'd know I'd lied, _____ oo.

⅏ Pre-Chorus

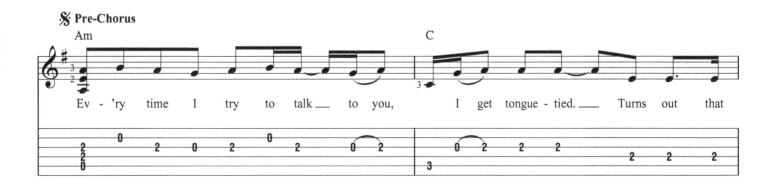

Ev - 'ry time I try to talk _ to you, I get tongue - tied. _ Turns out that

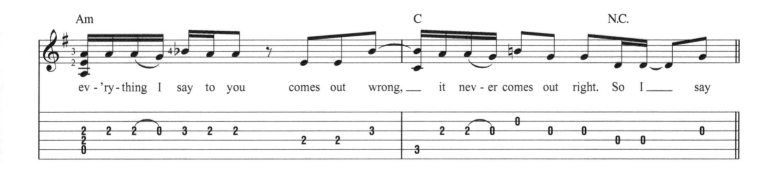

ev - 'ry- thing I say to you comes out wrong, _ it nev - er comes out right. So I _ say

Chorus

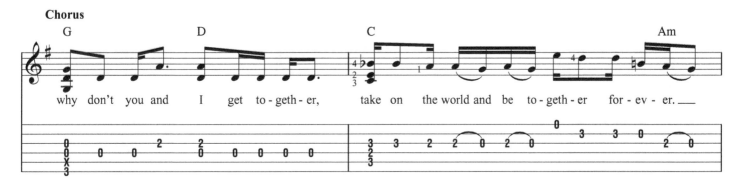

why don't you and I get to - geth - er, take on the world and be to - geth - er for - ev - er. _____

Heads, we will, tails, we'll try a - gain. __ So I say why don't you and I hold each oth- er,

3rd time, To Coda ⊕

fly to the moon and straight __ on to heav- en, 'cause with- out you, they're nev- er gon- na let me __ in. __

Bridge

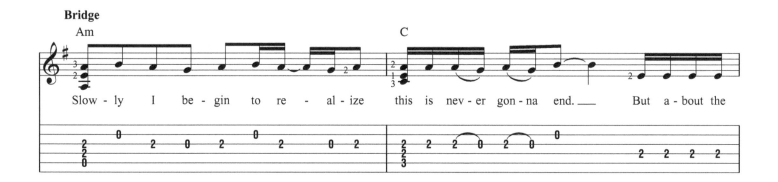

Slow - ly I be - gin to re - al - ize this is nev - er gon - na end. __ But a - bout the

same time you walk by, and I __ say, "Oh, here we go a - gain, oh."

Guitar Solo |1., 2., 3. ||4.   *D.S. al Coda*

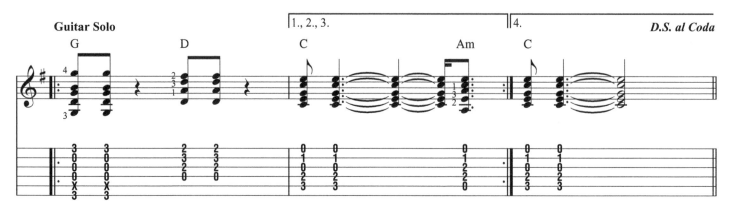

Coda

Guitar Solo

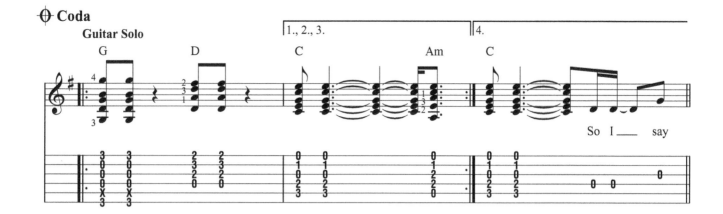

So I___ say

Outro-Chorus

why don't you and   I   get to-geth-er,   take on   the world and be   to-geth-er   for-ev-er.___

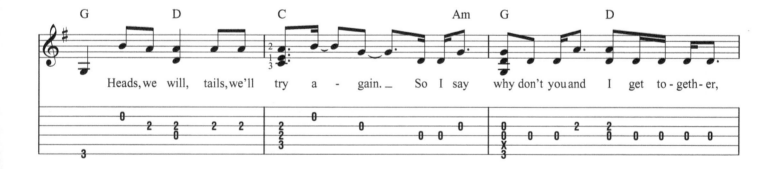

Heads, we will,   tails, we'll   try   a-gain.___   So I say   why don't you and   I   get to-geth-er,

Repeat and fade

fly   to the moon and straight _ on to heav-en,   'cause with-out you, they're nev-er gon-na   let   me _ in. _ So I ___ say

Additional Lyrics

2. When's this fever gonna break?
   I think I've handled more than any man can take.
   I'm like a love-sick puppy chasing you around,
   Oo, and it's alright.
   Bouncin' 'round from cloud to cloud,
   I got the feelin' like I'm never gonna come down.
   If I said I didn't like it then you'd know I'd lied, oo,

Put Your Lights On

Words and Music by Erik Schrody

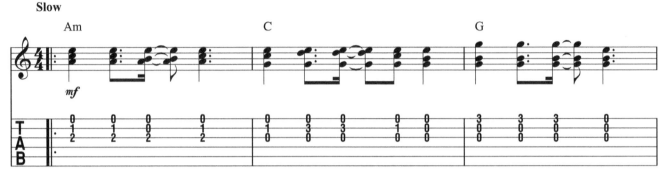

Strum Pattern: 5
Pick Pattern: 5

Intro
Slow

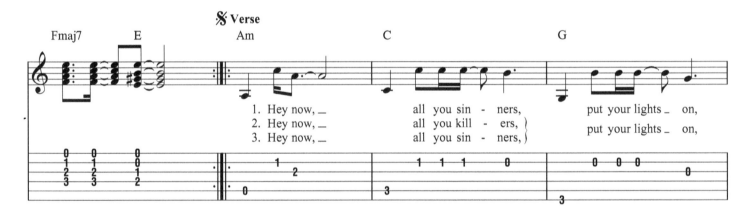

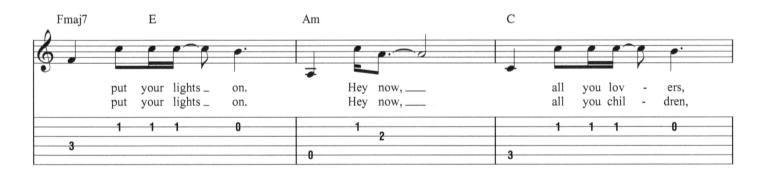

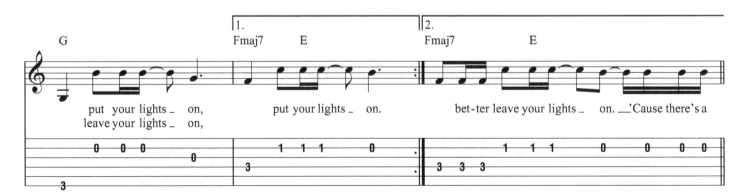

Lyrics:

1. Hey now, __ all you sin - ners, put your lights __ on,
2. Hey now, __ all you kill - ers, put your lights __ on,
3. Hey now, __ all you sin - ners,

put your lights __ on.
put your lights __ on.

Hey now, ___ all you lov - ers,
Hey now, ___ all you chil - dren,

put your lights __ on,
leave your lights __ on,

put your lights __ on.

bet-ter leave your lights __ on. __ 'Cause there's a

mon - ster   liv - in' un - der my bed,   a whis-per - in' in my

To Coda ⊕

ear,   and there's an an - gel   with a hand on my head,

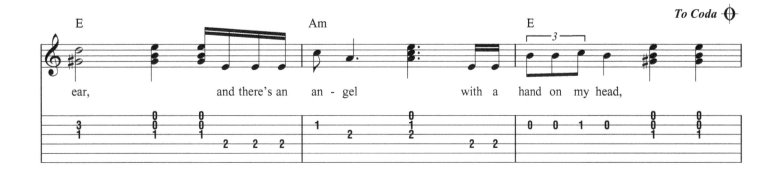

she say I got noth - in' to fear.   There's a dark - ness   liv - in'

deep in my soul.   I still got a pur-pose to serve.   So let your

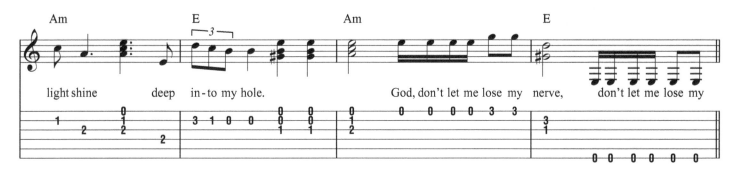

light shine   deep in-to my hole.   God, don't let me lose my nerve,   don't let me lose my

Guitar Solo

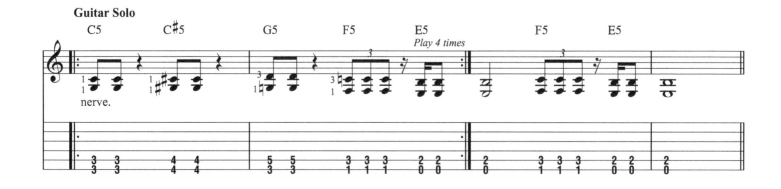

Interlude

2nd time, D.S. al Coda
(take 2nd ending)

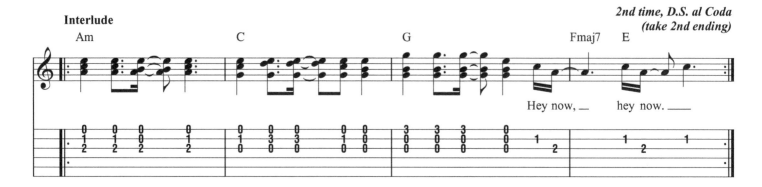

Hey now, — hey now. —

Coda   **Outro**

she say I got noth-in' to fear. She say, "Lá — il - á -

- ha — ill - al - láh." We all shine like stars.

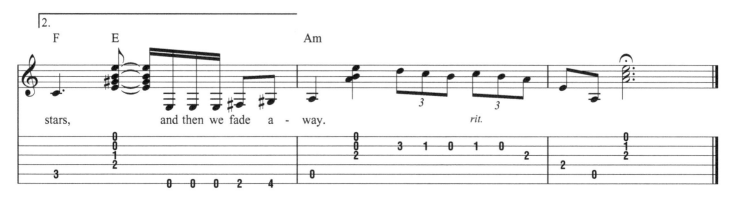

stars, and then we fade a - way.

This series features simplified arrangements with notes, tab, chord charts, and strum and pick patterns.

MIXED FOLIOS

00702287	Acoustic	$19.99
00702002	Acoustic Rock Hits for Easy Guitar	$15.99
00702166	All-Time Best Guitar Collection	$19.99
00702232	Best Acoustic Songs for Easy Guitar	$16.99
00119835	Best Children's Songs	$16.99
00703055	The Big Book of Nursery Rhymes & Children's Songs	$16.99
00698978	Big Christmas Collection	$19.99
00702394	Bluegrass Songs for Easy Guitar	$15.99
00289632	Bohemian Rhapsody	$19.99
00703387	Celtic Classics	$14.99
00224808	Chart Hits of 2016-2017	$14.99
00267383	Chart Hits of 2017-2018	$14.99
00334293	Chart Hits of 2019-2020	$16.99
00702149	Children's Christian Songbook	$9.99
00702028	Christmas Classics	$8.99
00101779	Christmas Guitar	$14.99
00702141	Classic Rock	$8.95
00159642	Classical Melodies	$12.99
00253933	Disney/Pixar's Coco	$16.99
00702203	CMT's 100 Greatest Country Songs	$34.99
00702283	The Contemporary Christian Collection	$16.99
00196954	Contemporary Disney	$19.99
00702239	Country Classics for Easy Guitar	$24.99
00702257	Easy Acoustic Guitar Songs	$16.99
00702041	Favorite Hymns for Easy Guitar	$12.99
00222701	Folk Pop Songs	$17.99
00126894	Frozen	$14.99
00333922	Frozen 2	$14.99
00702286	Glee	$16.99
00702160	The Great American Country Songbook	$19.99
00702148	Great American Gospel for Guitar	$14.99
00702050	Great Classical Themes for Easy Guitar	$9.99
00275088	The Greatest Showman	$17.99
00148030	Halloween Guitar Songs	$14.99
00702273	Irish Songs	$12.99
00192503	Jazz Classics for Easy Guitar	$16.99
00702275	Jazz Favorites for Easy Guitar	$17.99
00702274	Jazz Standards for Easy Guitar	$19.99
00702162	Jumbo Easy Guitar Songbook	$24.99
00232285	La La Land	$16.99
00702258	Legends of Rock	$14.99
00702189	MTV's 100 Greatest Pop Songs	$34.99
00702272	1950s Rock	$16.99
00702271	1960s Rock	$16.99
00702270	1970s Rock	$19.99
00702269	1980s Rock	$15.99
00702268	1990s Rock	$19.99
00369043	Rock Songs for Kids	$14.99
00109725	Once	$14.99
00702187	Selections from O Brother Where Art Thou?	$19.99
00702178	100 Songs for Kids	$14.99
00702515	Pirates of the Caribbean	$17.99
00702125	Praise and Worship for Guitar	$14.99
00287930	Songs from *A Star Is Born, The Greatest Showman, La La Land*, and More Movie Musicals	$16.99
00702285	Southern Rock Hits	$12.99
00156420	Star Wars Music	$16.99
00121535	30 Easy Celtic Guitar Solos	$16.99
00702156	3-Chord Rock	$12.99
00244654	Top Hits of 2017	$14.99
00283786	Top Hits of 2018	$14.99
00702294	Top Worship Hits	$17.99
00702255	VH1's 100 Greatest Hard Rock Songs	$34.99
00702175	VH1's 100 Greatest Songs of Rock and Roll	$29.99
00702253	Wicked	$12.99

ARTIST COLLECTIONS

00702267	AC/DC for Easy Guitar	$16.99
00702598	Adele for Easy Guitar	$15.99
00156221	Adele – 25	$16.99
00702040	Best of the Allman Brothers	$16.99
00702865	J.S. Bach for Easy Guitar	$15.99
00702169	Best of The Beach Boys	$15.99
00702292	The Beatles — 1	$22.99
00125796	Best of Chuck Berry	$15.99
00702201	The Essential Black Sabbath	$15.99
00702250	blink-182 — Greatest Hits	$17.99
02501615	Zac Brown Band — The Foundation	$17.99
02501621	Zac Brown Band — You Get What You Give	$16.99
00702043	Best of Johnny Cash	$17.99
00702090	Eric Clapton's Best	$16.99
00702086	Eric Clapton — from the Album Unplugged	$17.99
00702202	The Essential Eric Clapton	$17.99
00702053	Best of Patsy Cline	$15.99
00222697	Very Best of Coldplay – 2nd Edition	$16.99
00702229	The Very Best of Creedence Clearwater Revival	$16.99
00702145	Best of Jim Croce	$16.99
00702278	Crosby, Stills & Nash	$12.99
14042809	Bob Dylan	$15.99
00702276	Fleetwood Mac — Easy Guitar Collection	$17.99
00139462	The Very Best of Grateful Dead	$16.99
00702136	Best of Merle Haggard	$16.99
00702227	Jimi Hendrix — Smash Hits	$19.99
00702288	Best of Hillsong United	$12.99
00702236	Best of Antonio Carlos Jobim	$15.99
00702245	Elton John — Greatest Hits 1970–2002	$19.99
00129855	Jack Johnson	$16.99
00702204	Robert Johnson	$14.99
00702234	Selections from Toby Keith — 35 Biggest Hits	$12.95
00702003	Kiss	$16.99
00702216	Lynyrd Skynyrd	$16.99
00702182	The Essential Bob Marley	$16.99
00146081	Maroon 5	$14.99
00121925	Bruno Mars – Unorthodox Jukebox	$12.99
00702248	Paul McCartney — All the Best	$14.99
00125484	The Best of MercyMe	$12.99
00702209	Steve Miller Band — Young Hearts (Greatest Hits)	$12.95
00124167	Jason Mraz	$15.99
00702096	Best of Nirvana	$16.99
00702211	The Offspring — Greatest Hits	$17.99
00138026	One Direction	$17.99
00702030	Best of Roy Orbison	$17.99
00702144	Best of Ozzy Osbourne	$14.99
00702279	Tom Petty	$17.99
00102911	Pink Floyd	$17.99
00702139	Elvis Country Favorites	$19.99
00702293	The Very Best of Prince	$19.99
00699415	Best of Queen for Guitar	$16.99
00109279	Best of R.E.M.	$14.99
00702208	Red Hot Chili Peppers — Greatest Hits	$16.99
00198960	The Rolling Stones	$17.99
00174793	The Very Best of Santana	$16.99
00702196	Best of Bob Seger	$16.99
00146046	Ed Sheeran	$15.99
00702252	Frank Sinatra — Nothing But the Best	$12.99
00702010	Best of Rod Stewart	$17.99
00702049	Best of George Strait	$17.99
00702259	Taylor Swift for Easy Guitar	$15.99
00359800	Taylor Swift – Easy Guitar Anthology	$24.99
00702260	Taylor Swift — Fearless	$14.99
00139727	Taylor Swift — 1989	$17.99
00115960	Taylor Swift — Red	$16.99
00253667	Taylor Swift — Reputation	$17.99
00702290	Taylor Swift — Speak Now	$16.99
00232849	Chris Tomlin Collection – 2nd Edition	$14.99
00702226	Chris Tomlin — See the Morning	$12.95
00148643	Train	$14.99
00702427	U2 — 18 Singles	$19.99
00702108	Best of Stevie Ray Vaughan	$17.99
00279005	The Who	$14.99
00702123	Best of Hank Williams	$15.99
00194548	Best of John Williams	$14.99
00702228	Neil Young — Greatest Hits	$17.99
00119133	Neil Young — Harvest	$14.99

Prices, contents and availability subject to change without notice.

HAL•LEONARD®

Visit Hal Leonard online at **halleonard.com**

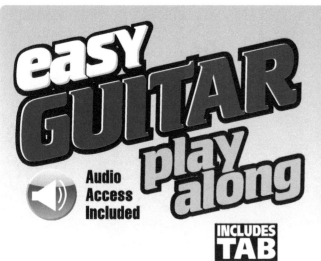

easy GUITAR play along

Audio Access Included

INCLUDES TAB

The **Easy Guitar Play Along®** series features streamlined transcriptions of your favorite songs. Just follow the tab, listen to the audio to hear how the guitar should sound, and then play along using the backing tracks. Playback tools are provided for slowing down the tempo without changing pitch and looping challenging parts. The melody and lyrics are included in the book so that you can sing or simply follow along.

1. ROCK CLASSICS
Jailbreak • Living After Midnight • Mississippi Queen • Rocks Off • Runnin' Down a Dream • Smoke on the Water • Strutter • Up Around the Bend.
00702560 Book/CD Pack....... $14.99

2. ACOUSTIC TOP HITS
About a Girl • I'm Yours • The Lazy Song • The Scientist • 21 Guns • Upside Down • What I Got • Wonderwall.
00702569 Book/CD Pack....... $14.99

3. ROCK HITS
All the Small Things • Best of You • Brain Stew (The Godzilla Remix) • Californication • Island in the Sun • Plush • Smells Like Teen Spirit • Use Somebody.
00702570 Book/CD Pack....... $14.99

4. ROCK 'N' ROLL
Blue Suede Shoes • I Get Around • I'm a Believer • Jailhouse Rock • Oh, Pretty Woman • Peggy Sue • Runaway • Wake Up Little Susie.
00702572 Book/CD Pack....... $14.99

6. CHRISTMAS SONGS
Have Yourself a Merry Little Christmas • A Holly Jolly Christmas • The Little Drummer Boy • Run Rudolph Run • Santa Claus Is Comin' to Town • Silver and Gold • Sleigh Ride • Winter Wonderland.
00101879 Book/CD Pack......... $14.99

7. BLUES SONGS FOR BEGINNERS
Come On (Part 1) • Double Trouble • Gangster of Love • I'm Ready • Let Me Love You Baby • Mary Had a Little Lamb • San-Ho-Zay • T-Bone Shuffle.
00103235 Book/
        Online Audio..........$17.99

9. ROCK SONGS FOR BEGINNERS
Are You Gonna Be My Girl • Buddy Holly • Everybody Hurts • In Bloom • Otherside • The Rock Show • Santa Monica • When I Come Around.
00103255 Book/CD Pack.....$14.99

10. GREEN DAY
Basket Case • Boulevard of Broken Dreams • Good Riddance (Time of Your Life) • Holiday • Longview • 21 Guns • Wake Me up When September Ends • When I Come Around.
00122322 Book/
        Online Audio $16.99

11. NIRVANA
All Apologies • Come As You Are • Heart Shaped Box • Lake of Fire • Lithium • The Man Who Sold the World • Rape Me • Smells Like Teen Spirit.
00122325 Book/
        Online Audio $17.99

13. AC/DC
Back in Black • Dirty Deeds Done Dirt Cheap • For Those About to Rock (We Salute You) • Hells Bells • Highway to Hell • Rock and Roll Ain't Noise Pollution • T.N.T. • You Shook Me All Night Long.
14042895 Book/
        Online Audio........ $17.99

14. JIMI HENDRIX – SMASH HITS
All Along the Watchtower • Can You See Me • Crosstown Traffic • Fire • Foxey Lady • Hey Joe • Manic Depression • Purple Haze • Red House • Remember • Stone Free • The Wind Cries Mary.
00130591 Book/
        Online Audio........$24.99

HAL•LEONARD®
www.halleonard.com

Prices, contents, and availability subject to change without notice.

HAL•LEONARD®

GUITAR PLAY-ALONG

Complete song lists available online.

This series will help you play your favorite songs quickly and easily. Just follow the tab and listen to the audio to the hear how the guitar should sound, and then play along using the separate backing tracks. Audio files also include software to slow down the tempo without changing pitch. The melody and lyrics are included in the book so that you can sing or simply follow along.

INCLUDES TAB

VOL. 1 – ROCK .... 00699570 / $17.99
VOL. 2 – ACOUSTIC .... 00699569 / $16.99
VOL. 3 – HARD ROCK .... 00699573 / $17.99
VOL. 4 – POP/ROCK .... 00699571 / $16.99
VOL. 5 – THREE CHORD SONGS .... 00300985 / $16.99
VOL. 6 – '90S ROCK .... 00298615 / $16.99
VOL. 7 – BLUES .... 00699575 / $19.99
VOL. 8 – ROCK .... 00699585 / $16.99
VOL. 9 – EASY ACOUSTIC SONGS .... 00151708 / $16.99
VOL. 10 – ACOUSTIC .... 00699586 / $16.95
VOL. 11 – EARLY ROCK .... 00699579 / $15.99
VOL. 12 – ROCK POP .... 00291724 / $16.99
VOL. 14 – BLUES ROCK .... 00699582 / $16.99
VOL. 15 – R&B .... 00699583 / $17.99
VOL. 16 – JAZZ .... 00699584 / $16.99
VOL. 17 – COUNTRY .... 00699588 / $17.99
VOL. 18 – ACOUSTIC ROCK .... 00699577 / $15.95
VOL. 20 – ROCKABILLY .... 00699580 / $17.99
VOL. 21 – SANTANA .... 00174525 / $17.99
VOL. 22 – CHRISTMAS .... 00699600 / $15.99
VOL. 23 – SURF .... 00699635 / $17.99
VOL. 24 – ERIC CLAPTON .... 00699649 / $19.99
VOL. 25 – THE BEATLES .... 00198265 / $19.99
VOL. 26 – ELVIS PRESLEY .... 00699643 / $16.99
VOL. 27 – DAVID LEE ROTH .... 00699645 / $16.95
VOL. 28 – GREG KOCH .... 00699646 / $19.99
VOL. 29 – BOB SEGER .... 00699647 / $16.99
VOL. 30 – KISS .... 00699644 / $17.99
VOL. 32 – THE OFFSPRING .... 00699653 / $14.95
VOL. 33 – ACOUSTIC CLASSICS .... 00699656 / $19.99
VOL. 34 – CLASSIC ROCK .... 00699658 / $17.99
VOL. 35 – HAIR METAL .... 00699660 / $17.99
VOL. 36 – SOUTHERN ROCK .... 00699661 / $19.99
VOL. 37 – ACOUSTIC UNPLUGGED .... 00699662 / $22.99
VOL. 38 – BLUES .... 00699663 / $17.99
VOL. 39 – '80s METAL .... 00699664 / $17.99
VOL. 40 – INCUBUS .... 00699668 / $17.95
VOL. 41 – ERIC CLAPTON .... 00699669 / $17.99
VOL. 42 – COVER BAND HITS .... 00211597 / $16.99
VOL. 43 – LYNYRD SKYNYRD .... 00699681 / $22.99
VOL. 44 – JAZZ GREATS .... 00699689 / $16.99
VOL. 45 – TV THEMES .... 00699718 / $14.95
VOL. 46 – MAINSTREAM ROCK .... 00699722 / $16.95
VOL. 47 – JIMI HENDRIX SMASH HITS .... 00699723 / $19.99
VOL. 48 – AEROSMITH CLASSICS .... 00699724 / $17.99
VOL. 49 – STEVIE RAY VAUGHAN .... 00699725 / $17.99
VOL. 50 – VAN HALEN: 1978-1984 .... 00110269 / $19.99
VOL. 51 – ALTERNATIVE '90s .... 00699727 / $14.99
VOL. 52 – FUNK .... 00699728 / $15.99
VOL. 53 – DISCO .... 00699729 / $14.99
VOL. 54 – HEAVY METAL .... 00699730 / $17.99
VOL. 55 – POP METAL .... 00699731 / $14.95
VOL. 57 – GUNS 'N' ROSES .... 00159922 / $19.99
VOL. 58 – BLINK 182 .... 00699772 / $17.99
VOL. 59 – CHET ATKINS .... 00702347 / $17.99
VOL. 60 – 3 DOORS DOWN .... 00699774 / $14.95
VOL. 62 – CHRISTMAS CAROLS .... 00699798 / $12.95
VOL. 63 – CREEDENCE CLEARWATER REVIVAL .... 00699802 / $17.99
VOL. 64 – ULTIMATE OZZY OSBOURNE .... 00699803 / $19.99
VOL. 66 – THE ROLLING STONES .... 00699807 / $19.99
VOL. 67 – BLACK SABBATH .... 00699808 / $17.99
VOL. 68 – PINK FLOYD – DARK SIDE OF THE MOON .... 00699809 / $17.99
VOL. 71 – CHRISTIAN ROCK .... 00699824 / $14.95
VOL. 73 – BLUESY ROCK .... 00699829 / $17.99
VOL. 74 – SIMPLE STRUMMING SONGS .... 00151706 / $19.99
VOL. 75 – TOM PETTY .... 00699882 / $19.99
VOL. 76 – COUNTRY HITS .... 00699884 / $16.99
VOL. 77 – BLUEGRASS .... 00699910 / $17.99
VOL. 78 – NIRVANA .... 00700132 / $17.99
VOL. 79 – NEIL YOUNG .... 00700133 / $24.99
VOL. 81 – ROCK ANTHOLOGY .... 00700176 / $22.99
VOL. 82 – EASY ROCK SONGS .... 00700177 / $17.99
VOL. 84 – STEELY DAN .... 00700200 / $19.99
VOL. 85 – THE POLICE .... 00700269 / $16.99
VOL. 86 – BOSTON .... 00700465 / $19.99
VOL. 87 – ACOUSTIC WOMEN .... 00700763 / $14.99
VOL. 88 – GRUNGE .... 00700467 / $16.99
VOL. 89 – REGGAE .... 00700468 / $15.99
VOL. 90 – CLASSICAL POP .... 00700469 / $14.99
VOL. 91 – BLUES INSTRUMENTALS .... 00700505 / $19.99
VOL. 92 – EARLY ROCK INSTRUMENTALS .... 00700506 / $17.99
VOL. 93 – ROCK INSTRUMENTALS .... 00700507 / $17.99
VOL. 94 – SLOW BLUES .... 00700508 / $16.99
VOL. 95 – BLUES CLASSICS .... 00700509 / $15.99
VOL. 96 – BEST COUNTRY HITS .... 00211615 / $16.99
VOL. 97 – CHRISTMAS CLASSICS .... 00236542 / $14.99
VOL. 99 – ZZ TOP .... 00700762 / $16.99
VOL. 100 – B.B. KING .... 00700466 / $16.99
VOL. 101 – SONGS FOR BEGINNERS .... 00701917 / $14.99
VOL. 102 – CLASSIC PUNK .... 00700769 / $14.99
VOL. 104 – DUANE ALLMAN .... 00700846 / $22.99
VOL. 105 – LATIN .... 00700939 / $16.99
VOL. 106 – WEEZER .... 00700958 / $17.99
VOL. 107 – CREAM .... 00701069 / $17.99
VOL. 108 – THE WHO .... 00701053 / $17.99
VOL. 109 – STEVE MILLER .... 00701054 / $19.99
VOL. 110 – SLIDE GUITAR HITS .... 00701055 / $17.99
VOL. 111 – JOHN MELLENCAMP .... 00701056 / $14.99
VOL. 112 – QUEEN .... 00701052 / $16.99
VOL. 113 – JIM CROCE .... 00701058 / $19.99
VOL. 114 – BON JOVI .... 00701060 / $17.99
VOL. 115 – JOHNNY CASH .... 00701070 / $17.99
VOL. 116 – THE VENTURES .... 00701124 / $17.99
VOL. 117 – BRAD PAISLEY .... 00701224 / $16.99
VOL. 118 – ERIC JOHNSON .... 00701353 / $17.99
VOL. 119 – AC/DC CLASSICS .... 00701356 / $19.99
VOL. 120 – PROGRESSIVE ROCK .... 00701457 / $14.99
VOL. 121 – U2 .... 00701508 / $17.99
VOL. 122 – CROSBY, STILLS & NASH .... 00701610 / $16.99
VOL. 123 – LENNON & McCARTNEY ACOUSTIC .... 00701614 / $16.99
VOL. 124 – SMOOTH JAZZ .... 00200664 / $16.99
VOL. 125 – JEFF BECK .... 00701687 / $19.99
VOL. 126 – BOB MARLEY .... 00701701 / $17.99
VOL. 127 – 1970s ROCK .... 00701739 / $17.99
VOL. 128 – 1960s ROCK .... 00701740 / $14.99
VOL. 129 – MEGADETH .... 00701741 / $17.99
VOL. 130 – IRON MAIDEN .... 00701742 / $17.99
VOL. 131 – 1990s ROCK .... 00701743 / $14.99
VOL. 132 – COUNTRY ROCK .... 00701757 / $15.99
VOL. 133 – TAYLOR SWIFT .... 00701894 / $16.99
VOL. 135 – MINOR BLUES .... 00151350 / $17.99
VOL. 136 – GUITAR THEMES .... 00701922 / $14.99
VOL. 137 – IRISH TUNES .... 00701966 / $15.99
VOL. 138 – BLUEGRASS CLASSICS .... 00701967 / $17.99
VOL. 139 – GARY MOORE .... 00702370 / $17.99
VOL. 140 – MORE STEVIE RAY VAUGHAN .... 00702396 / $19.99
VOL. 141 – ACOUSTIC HITS .... 00702401 / $16.99
VOL. 142 – GEORGE HARRISON .... 00237697 / $17.99
VOL. 143 – SLASH .... 00702425 / $19.99
VOL. 144 – DJANGO REINHARDT .... 00702531 / $17.99
VOL. 145 – DEF LEPPARD .... 00702532 / $19.99
VOL. 146 – ROBERT JOHNSON .... 00702533 / $16.99
VOL. 147 – SIMON & GARFUNKEL .... 14041591 / $17.99
VOL. 148 – BOB DYLAN .... 14041592 / $17.99
VOL. 149 – AC/DC HITS .... 14041593 / $19.99
VOL. 150 – ZAKK WYLDE .... 02501717 / $19.99
VOL. 151 – J.S. BACH .... 02501730 / $16.99
VOL. 152 – JOE BONAMASSA .... 02501751 / $24.99
VOL. 153 – RED HOT CHILI PEPPERS .... 00702990 / $22.99
VOL. 155 – ERIC CLAPTON UNPLUGGED .... 00703085 / $17.99
VOL. 156 – SLAYER .... 00703770 / $19.99
VOL. 157 – FLEETWOOD MAC .... 00101382 / $17.99
VOL. 159 – WES MONTGOMERY .... 00102593 / $22.99
VOL. 160 – T-BONE WALKER 00102641/ $17.99
VOL. 161 – THE EAGLES ACOUSTIC .... 00102659 / $19.99
VOL. 162 – THE EAGLES HITS .... 00102667 / $17.99
VOL. 163 – PANTERA .... 00103036 / $19.99
VOL. 164 – VAN HALEN: 1986-1995 .... 00110270 / $19.99
VOL. 165 – GREEN DAY .... 00210343 / $17.99
VOL. 166 – MODERN BLUES .... 00700764 / $16.99
VOL. 167 – DREAM THEATER .... 00111938 / $24.99
VOL. 168 – KISS .... 00113421 / $17.99
VOL. 169 – TAYLOR SWIFT .... 00115982 / $16.99
VOL. 170 – THREE DAYS GRACE .... 00117337 / $16.99
VOL. 171 – JAMES BROWN .... 00117420 / $16.99
VOL. 172 – THE DOOBIE BROTHERS .... 00119670 / $17.99
VOL. 173 – TRANS-SIBERIAN ORCHESTRA .... 00119907 / $19.99
VOL. 174 – SCORPIONS .... 00122119 / $19.99
VOL. 175 – MICHAEL SCHENKER .... 00122127 / $17.99
VOL. 176 – BLUES BREAKERS WITH JOHN MAYALL & ERIC CLAPTON .... 00122132 / $19.99
VOL. 177 – ALBERT KING .... 00123271 / $17.99
VOL. 178 – JASON MRAZ .... 00124165 / $17.99
VOL. 179 – RAMONES .... 00127073 / $16.99
VOL. 180 – BRUNO MARS .... 00129706 / $16.99
VOL. 181 – JACK JOHNSON .... 00129854 / $16.99
VOL. 182 – SOUNDGARDEN .... 00138161 / $17.99
VOL. 183 – BUDDY GUY .... 00138240 / $17.99
VOL. 184 – KENNY WAYNE SHEPHERD .... 00138258 / $17.99
VOL. 185 – JOE SATRIANI .... 00139457 / $19.99
VOL. 186 – GRATEFUL DEAD .... 00139459 / $17.99
VOL. 187 – JOHN DENVER .... 00140839 / $19.99
VOL. 188 – MÖTLEY CRÜE .... 00141145 / $19.99
VOL. 189 – JOHN MAYER .... 00144350 / $19.99
VOL. 190 – DEEP PURPLE .... 00146152 / $19.99
VOL. 191 – PINK FLOYD CLASSICS .... 00146164 / $17.99
VOL. 192 – JUDAS PRIEST .... 00151352 / $19.99
VOL. 193 – STEVE VAI .... 00156028 / $19.99
VOL. 194 – PEARL JAM .... 00157925 / $17.99
VOL. 195 – METALLICA: 1983-1988 .... 00234291 / $22.99
VOL. 196 – METALLICA: 1991-2016 .... 00234292 / $19.99

Prices, contents, and availability subject to change without notice.

HAL•LEONARD®
www.halleonard.com

0222
173

GUITAR *signature licks*

Signature Licks book/audio packs provide a step-by-step breakdown of "right from the record" riffs, licks, and solos so you can jam along with your favorite bands. They contain performance notes and an overview of each artist's or group's style, with note-for-note transcriptions in notes and tab. The online audio tracks feature full-band demos at both normal and slow speeds.

AC/DC
14041352 .... $24.99

AEROSMITH 1973-1979
00695106 .... $24.99

AEROSMITH 1979-1998
00695219 .... $22.95

DUANE ALLMAN
00696042 .... $22.99

BEST OF CHET ATKINS
00695752 .... $24.99

AVENGED SEVENFOLD
00696473 .... $24.99

THE BEATLES
00298845 .... $24.99

BEST OF THE BEATLES FOR ACOUSTIC GUITAR
00695453 .... $24.99

THE BEATLES HITS
00695049 .... $24.95

JEFF BECK
00696427 .... $24.99

BEST OF GEORGE BENSON
00695418 .... $22.99

BEST OF BLACK SABBATH
00695249 .... $24.99

BLUES BREAKERS WITH JOHN MAYALL & ERIC CLAPTON
00696374 .... $24.99

BON JOVI
00696380 .... $22.99

ROY BUCHANAN
00696654 .... $22.99

KENNY BURRELL
00695830 .... $27.99

BEST OF CHARLIE CHRISTIAN
00695584 .... $24.99

BEST OF ERIC CLAPTON
00695038 .... $24.99

ERIC CLAPTON – FROM THE ALBUM UNPLUGGED
00695250 .... $24.99

BEST OF CREAM
00695251 .... $24.99

THE DOORS
00695373 .... $22.95

DEEP PURPLE – GREATEST HITS
00695625 .... $24.99

DREAM THEATER
00111943 .... $24.99

TOMMY EMMANUEL
00696409 .... $22.99

ESSENTIAL JAZZ GUITAR
00695875 .... $19.99

FLEETWOOD MAC
00696416 .... $22.99

ROBBEN FORD
00695903 .... $22.95

BEST OF GRANT GREEN
00695747 .... $24.99

PETER GREEN
00145386 .... $24.99

BEST OF GUNS N' ROSES
00695183 .... $24.99

THE BEST OF BUDDY GUY
00695186 .... $22.99

JIM HALL
00695848 .... $29.99

JIMI HENDRIX
00696560 .... $24.99

JIMI HENDRIX – VOLUME 2
00695835 .... $24.99

JOHN LEE HOOKER
00695894 .... $22.99

BEST OF JAZZ GUITAR
00695586 .... $29.99

ERIC JOHNSON
00699317 .... $24.99

ROBERT JOHNSON
00695264 .... $24.99

BARNEY KESSEL
00696009 .... $24.99

THE ESSENTIAL ALBERT KING
00695713 .... $24.99

B.B. KING – BLUES LEGEND
00696039 .... $22.99

B.B. KING – THE DEFINITIVE COLLECTION
00695635 .... $22.99

MARK KNOPFLER
00695178 .... $24.99

LYNYRD SKYNYRD
00695872 .... $24.99

THE BEST OF YNGWIE MALMSTEEN
00695669 .... $24.99

BEST OF PAT MARTINO
00695632 .... $24.99

MEGADETH
00696421 .... $22.99

WES MONTGOMERY
00695387 .... $24.99

BEST OF NIRVANA
00695483 .... $24.95

VERY BEST OF OZZY OSBOURNE
00695431 .... $22.99

BRAD PAISLEY
00696379 .... $22.99

BEST OF JOE PASS
00695730 .... $24.99

TOM PETTY
00696021 .... $24.99

PINK FLOYD
00103659 .... $27.99

THE GUITARS OF ELVIS
00174800 .... $22.99

BEST OF QUEEN
00695097 .... $24.99

RADIOHEAD
00109304 .... $24.99

BEST OF RAGE AGAINST THE MACHINE
00695480 .... $24.99

JERRY REED
00118236 .... $22.99

BEST OF DJANGO REINHARDT
00695660 .... $27.99

BEST OF ROCK 'N' ROLL GUITAR
00695559 .... $24.99

BEST OF ROCKABILLY GUITAR
00695785 .... $19.99

BEST OF CARLOS SANTANA
00174664 .... $22.99

BEST OF JOE SATRIANI
00695216 .... $24.99

SLASH
00696576 .... $22.99

SLAYER
00121281 .... $22.99

BEST OF SOUTHERN ROCK
00695560 .... $19.95

STEELY DAN
00696015 .... $22.99

MIKE STERN
00695800 .... $27.99

BEST OF SURF GUITAR
00695822 .... $22.99

STEVE VAI
00673247 .... $24.99

STEVE VAI – ALIEN LOVE SECRETS: THE NAKED VAMPS
00695223 .... $22.95

STEVE VAI – FIRE GARDEN: THE NAKED VAMPS
00695166 .... $22.95

STEVE VAI – THE ULTRA ZONE: NAKED VAMPS
00695684 .... $22.95

VAN HALEN
00110227 .... $24.99

THE GUITAR STYLE OF STEVIE RAY VAUGHAN
00695155 .... $24.95

BEST OF THE VENTURES
00695772 .... $24.99

THE WHO – 2ND ED.
00695561 .... $22.95

JOHNNY WINTER
00695951 .... $24.99

YES
00113120 .... $24.99

NEIL YOUNG – GREATEST HITS
00695988 .... $24.99

BEST OF ZZ TOP
00695738 .... $24.99